The Time Diet
Time Management for College Survival

D0061068

Emily Schwartz

To college students everywhere. You can do it!

CONTENTS

ACKNOWLEDGMENTS

This book would not be possible without the help of some very special people. First and foremost, my husband, Dan, who is my daily inspiration and the biggest cheerleader of everything I do. Also to my mom, dad, sister, and every teacher I ever had who always encouraged me to do well in school and taught me that hard work always pays off. I was fortunate to have an amazing editor, Susan Leon, who helped take a rough manuscript and really make it shine. Finally, thank you to Heather, my college roommate for four years and dear friend. My wish for all my readers is to have as good a friend to ride with down the bumpy road of college as I did.

Emily Schwartz

INTRODUCTION

Emily Schwartz

One evening, I arrived at one of my master's degree classes extra early. Even though I was exhausted from my fulltime job of teaching elementary school band, it was my group's turn to do our presentation and I wanted to make sure our PowerPoint was working correctly. (No, I'm sorry to report, group projects don't end after high school.) The semester had been particularly hectic since, in addition to teaching, I was also working a second part-time job taking catering orders for a grocery store, enrolled in two college classes, preparing for the upcoming holidays and still getting used to living in a new state.

With all of this going on, preparing for this end-of-semester project could have easily overwhelmed me. In fact, when my professor first assigned it, I was a little worried that I might not actually have time to get it done and do a good job. I sat down with my planner and mapped out exactly when I would work on this project so that I would have time to finish it without pulling an all-nighter the night before the deadline. Sometimes the only time during the week I could devote to this project was on a Saturday afternoon, which meant giving up my favorite yoga class at the gym, or meeting my friends for lunch. Sometimes I needed to stay up an hour or two later than usual to make sure I didn't get behind. It was a lot of work, but sure enough, I not only finished my part of the project by the deadline, but I finished it a few days early so I didn't need to stress about it.

Walking into class that night, I felt very proud. Who says working full time and going to school is hard? I can do it! I worked while pursuing my undergraduate degree and now I was working through graduate school. As I opened up my laptop, I saw that all of the connections were working, and my second group member arrived and helped me load her part of the presentation into my PowerPoint. All that was left was to wait for our third group member to show up and we'd be all set! The minutes ticked by as we waited for him to arrive. I started to get anxious. Where was he? Was there an event at the theater next door that was holding up traffic? Why didn't he

3

think about that and leave earlier? Other students in the class were starting to come in. Pretty soon the professor arrived and class was about to begin. My partner and I were frantically trying to call and text our third group member when he suddenly strolled through the door.

"Thank goodness!" I whispered loudly as he sat down next to us. "Where have you been?" My heart rate had finally started to slow back down to normal. "Here," I said as I started to hand him my laptop. "You can add your part to the presentation and we'll be all set."

"Dude," he responded while rubbing his temples with his fingertips in the most desperate, melodramatic attempt to look stressed out that I have ever seen. "I was soooo busy this week, I just didn't have time to finish it."

What followed was a barrage of excuses about why he wasn't able to work on it, but I wasn't listening. I was furious. Too busy?? Are you kidding me? Almost everyone in this class works full time and has lives outside of class. We're all busy but because we care about this class, we all make sacrifices and work hard to get our assignments done. Not only that, but this was a huge project! We'd known about it for a month! Half of our respective final grades were riding on this outcome and half of tonight's three-hour class was supposed to be dedicated to this presentation. What was he thinking? Did he think it was just going to get done by itself? I imagine that sometime in the last month he had watched at least an hour of television, IM'd with his friends or checked his Facebook wall. Was he really "too busy?"

I suppose part of it was my fault. I should have done a better job of checking in with him to make sure he was getting his part of our project done. I wrongly assumed that by the time people get to graduate school, they have learned a thing or two about time management. Well, so much for that idea.

With less than five minutes to go before we were supposed to start, we quickly figured out how we could make up for our flakey group member. We scanned through the existing parts of the presentation, found a few sections we could expand and took out the slides that were supposed to introduce the missing part of the presentation. It wasn't what we originally had planned, and maybe wasn't as complete and comprehensive as we knew it should be, but it would work. It took a little thinking-on-our-feet, but we made it through the presentation OK.

When I went home that evening, I vented my frustration to anyone who would listen and then pulled my laptop out and starting writing this book.

Why? Because I don't want any college student to either be that flakey group member or have to deal with that flakey group member ever again.

Time management in college does not need to be difficult. Students just need to stop making excuses and have a plan for getting their work done.

College Can be Overwhelming

Don't get me wrong, it's not like I don't understand where my flakey group member was coming from. College can be really overwhelming! Here you are trying to manage a class schedule, homework, a social life and maybe even a job all while getting used to living on your own for the first time and managing the new freedoms that come with that. It can be a lot to keep track of, especially if you don't know how. College isn't like you see in movies where a bunch of nineteen-year-olds party every night until the sun comes up and homework magically gets completed off-screen sometime. (Well, let's put it this way, it certainly isn't like that if you want to graduate and prepare yourself for your future!)

The sad truth is that graduating high school seniors are often terribly under-prepared to manage their time correctly. As much as we all hate to have our parents nag us, let's be honest with ourselves. In high school, sometimes parental nagging was the only thing that kept us on track! Would you really have chosen to work on your homework over the weekend if your mom hadn't made you? No! Teachers try to help you with time management by making you write down your homework in a planner and checking up on you during big projects to make sure you are hitting the benchmarks and aren't saving all your work for the last minute, but that isn't always enough. Sure, you get really good at learning to write things down in your planner, but time management is so much more than that. It's an attitude you have to learn, and that's what this book will help you acquire. When you have the right attitude about time management, you don't need someone checking up on you to make sure you're meeting your deadlines. You have the strength and discipline to do it on your own.

The Time Diet

It's time to start changing the way you think about time management. Your success in college depends on it. It's all very logical. Think about it: When people feel they are carrying around too much weight, they go on a diet and start making healthy choices about what they eat every day. When you enter college and feel like your schedule is overwhelming and weighing you down, you go on a Time Diet. The Time Diet is all about making smart choices with your time to complete everything for school while still making time for the fun things you want to do that enrich the college experience and make memories. Imagine: never having to pull an all-nighter ever again, never having to stare down your schedule during finals and wonder how in the world you will ever survive, never feeling the anxiety of failure because you aren't ready, never having to practice an excuse in the mirror before going to class and groveling for an extension.

As with a regular food diet, The Time Diet is all about control. When diets fail, it is because people still feel that the food is in control of them. The same is true for The Time Diet. The key to time management is realizing that only you are in control of your schedule. Nobody makes you do anything. Everything you do is a choice. You can choose to get things done efficiently or you can choose to waste your time and end up stressing out later. This book will teach you how to take control of the power you have to maximize your time and do all the things that are important to you.

How to Use This Book
This book is divided into three main parts:

> 1) The Right Attitude
> 2) The Nuts and Bolts of Organization
> 3) Getting it Done Faster

Most readers will be tempted to skip straight to Part Three. I urge you not to! Time management is a process. If you skip Parts One and Two, Part Three won't make sense. There is no one magic nugget of information in Part Three that will make you suddenly get your work done faster. You have to first get the right attitude about time management, then learn how to organize your time and then you can start accomplishing things more efficiently.

This book is filled with worksheets. You should fill them out either in your head, in the book itself or on a separate piece of paper. They are designed to help you apply the concepts in this book to your own personal situation. Sometimes just reading about something in a book only takes you so far. You have to actually figure out how you can apply it to your life before it becomes really useful.

Throughout this book, I will refer to "tasks" in your schedule that need to be completed. A task can be anything. It can be something that happens at a fixed time like going to class. It can be something that must be broken into smaller pieces and spread across several days like studying for a test. It can also be something small and easy like getting your laundry done (yes, in college you'll have to get that done too). Your daily schedule is made up of many different sized tasks that we must decide where to place. It's like a giant puzzle. The Time Diet helps you organize those tasks so that you can fit the most in your schedule and feel the best about what you've accomplished.

You Can Do It

Finally, I want to emphasize that even the very best students can feel overwhelmed by college sometimes. Don't let that get you down! It's all part of the college experience. Many, many students graduate from college and live to tell about it and so will you! When you feel as though you're drowning in stress, think of this guide as a trusty life preserver. You have the power and determination to succeed in college. This book will just give you some help and guidance along the way.

Now you're all ready to go! Happy reading, and be prepared to start taking control of your day. You will never look at time management the same way ever again.

PART 1
THE RIGHT ATTITUDE

Emily Schwartz

The first step to having excellent time management skills is having the right attitude. Time management has developed a little bit of a bad rap on college campuses. After all, by the time you enter college, you've already been in school for thirteen years or more. That is plenty of time to develop a bad attitude about managing your time. Perhaps when you hear the words "time management" the first image that pops into your head is that of your annoyed fifth grade teacher hunched over your desk berating you for not writing down your homework in your assignment calendar properly. It's no wonder by they time they get to college, students think that having good time management skills means being super organized, chaining yourself to your computer all day and never having any fun. I'm here to tell you that that's not time management. I've taken many false negative perceptions about time management and narrowed them down to five big myths that I am going to debunk one by one throughout this book.

Myth #1: Busy Equals Productive

People often think that as long as they are busy doing *something*, they are being productive with their time. I could stare at a word document on my computer screen all evening, but unless I've actually made progress on my paper, I've just been busy, not productive!

Myth #2: Your Schedule Controls You

It's easy to think that your class schedule and homework deadlines control you and that if you want to be a good student, you can't also have fun in college. This is not true. You control your schedule. Not the other way around. You can make time for both work and fun.

Myth #3: The Color-Coded Calendar is the Only Way

Have you ever seen those super organized to-do lists in which every minute is carefully scripted out? Every different kind of task is coded by color. Homework is in blue! Tests are in green! Meetings are in purple! You don't need a super-detailed system like this to have highly effective time management skills.

Myth #4 I Don't Have Time to Get it All Done

Half the stress of getting it all done comes from *worrying* about how you will get it all done! If we would all spend less time worrying and more time doing we'd be a lot more productive and far less stressed out.

Myth #5 I Must Stick to My To-Do List Exactly

Once you have the perfect to-do list set for your day, don't get upset when something unexpected happens that forces you to change your plan. Being flexible is important. Life happens! Printers break! Tires get nails in them! Being able to deal with day-to-day "mini crises" which disrupt your day is an important skill in time management.

Do any of these myths sound familiar? Maybe you've heard them from friends or caught yourself using them as an excuse to put off your work. Don't worry. Many college students (and graduates for that matter) believe these myths are true. After all, something is only called a "myth" if enough people actually pass it around as truth! However, now you know the secret. Throughout this book you'll hear more about these myths as we explore them, debunk them and ultimately change the way you think about them.

Thinking About It Differently

As I wrote in the introduction, the best way to start regaining control of your time management is to change your attitude and start thinking about time in a different way.

Thinking about it like a diet is a great way to stop seeing time management as something extra you have to do and to start making it a way of life that you can maintain even after college.

> ◈ Thinking of time management like a diet turns a dull concept into something more palatable and simplistic.

When people diet by eating nothing but fruits and vegetables all day, they may be able to last a few days or weeks, but pretty soon cravings for hamburgers, chocolate cake or other guilty pleasures become unbearable. Diets that produce more long-term results usually involve changing your lifestyle so that you eat a wide variety of foods you like in moderation. You may eat plenty of fruits and vegetables, but an occasional chocolate chip cookie doesn't kill you! The Time Diet works the same way. If you tell yourself that you're going to spend your weekends studying nonstop and never go out to have fun, you will eventually burn out. It's unrealistic to think you can work nonstop and still enjoy a healthy life. You need to adopt a lifestyle that involves getting your work done in chunks over a period of time so you can still have time to do the things you enjoy!

Choosing a Balanced Diet

Just as the products we consume are divided into different food groups, everything you do during the day can be divided into three different kinds of tasks:

1) **"Meats"** These are big, important, thinking-intensive tasks.
Some examples of Meats could be large projects, term papers and studying for big tests.

2) **"Vegetables"** These tasks are also important, but are smaller or less thinking-intensive than "meats." They are the fiber of college work.
Some examples of Vegetables could include weekly homework assignments, labs, making flashcards for studying and taking notes during reading assignments.

3) **"Desserts"** These are fun tasks we look forward to everyday.
Some examples of Desserts include hanging out with your friends, watching a favorite TV show, participating in a club, hobby or sport, hitting the gym or just taking a nap!

What Tasks Are In Your Food Groups?

Take a moment to think about the kinds of tasks you regularly do and separate them into the three categories. What are your.....

Meats	*An example of a meat task…*
Vegetables	*An example of a vegetable task…*
Desserts	*An example of a dessert task…*

A successful Time Diet will involve choosing tasks from all three of these categories. Once you have chosen the tasks you would like to do during a day, figure out which "food group" they all belong to. Did you make a balanced selection?

A schedule of mostly Meats will leave you feeling burnt out.
You can't expect yourself to work at the highest level of thinking for the entire day! You need to choose a few Meaty tasks you want to focus on during the day and intersperse them with other tasks.

Think about it: Have you ever given yourself two days to study for a big test, and then wondered why you are so burnt out you can't process all of the information? Studying for a big test is a Meat task. You wouldn't expect to feel too good if you ate nothing but steak for breakfast, lunch, and dinner for two entire days. (If that sounds delicious to you, try it, and let me know how it turns out.) That is essentially what you are doing to yourself when you schedule only Meat tasks for two days straight. Instead, you have to break up a Meaty task like studying for a final exam over the course of a week or more. Set aside a few hours each day of intense studying and you'll be far less overwhelmed and retain more information.

A schedule of only Vegetables will leave you feeling busy, not productive.
Have you ever had one of those days where you felt like you worked all day but didn't actually get anything done? You might be choosing too many Vegetables and not enough Meats. Big tasks will give your day direction and purpose.

I'm sure you've experienced those days when you've sat at your computer for a while only to look up at the clock, realize that three hours have passed and wonder, "Wait, what have I been doing all this time?!" Vegetable tasks, like lighter homework assignments or skimming through large chunks of assigned reading may at first seem like a good, easy way to spend the day, but they don't give you any sense of accomplishment. This is why people can only stay occupied with Vegetable tasks so long before their eyes start to glaze over and their minds start to wander. When this happens, they usually end up having to re-do the Vegetable task since they didn't really focus the first time. What a huge waste of time!

Vegetables are great and you should eat a lot of them, but if you eat carrots all day long, I'm betting you won't have a lot of energy in the late afternoon. You need meat, like a turkey sandwich or a cheeseburger to supplement all of those veggies. If you choose Vegetable tasks all day long it's hard to feel like you've actually done anything even though you've technically been "busy" all day. If a friend asked you what you did all day, you might have to think about it for a second: "What did I actually do today?" You need a few Meat tasks to give your day purpose.

Another problem with Vegetable tasks is we sometimes do them to avoid doing Meat tasks. Be honest: have you ever sat down to start a big project, and then eyed that enormous pile of papers scattered on your desk and said, "You know what? I'll start this project as soon as I finish organizing those papers....and hang up my clothes....and organize my sock drawer." We all do this! Try not to use Vegetable tasks as substitute time fillers for other more important things.

A schedule of only Desserts will leave you feeling lazy.
Every day needs a little fun to help you keep your sanity. Fun, Dessert tasks keep you happy and give your college life more excitement than doing homework all day will. Don't let anyone tell you that a huge part of college isn't about having fun and enjoying your transition into adulthood. This is the time to discover yourself, try new things, meet new friends and find out what you're good at.

However, a schedule of only Desserts will get you nowhere. It gets old after a while. Even lounging around with your friends in your dorm room can get boring. Pretty soon you'll need some stimulation, to use that good brain of yours that got you admitted to college in the first place. Besides, half of what makes Desserts so enjoyable is that they are a break from schoolwork. If you haven't done any work in a while to deserve your fun things, they seem less....well....fun! It's like when you were little, and you wished your birthday was every day but your mom said, "If your birthday were every day then it would never seem special and you wouldn't enjoy it." That mom. She was really on to something.

> ❖Don't forget to choose a balanced diet of tasks each day!

Making Good Choices

Think back to my story from the beginning of the book, the one where I worked really hard on a group project only to have another group member blow it off. Do you remember what his excuse was for not getting his work done? He was "too busy." He is what we call a "Busy Body." He has lots to do...and thinks he's the only one!

This brings us to Myth #1:

Myth #1: Busy Equals Productive

Just because you are filling hours in your day does not mean you are being productive! Understanding the difference between being "busy" and being "productive" is essential before you begin your Time Diet. "Busy" simply means that you are occupying your time. "Productive" means you are making concrete progress toward a goal. Students who are concerned with being productive are successful. Students who are concerned with being busy become a "Busy Body." Busy Bodies love to have lots to do. It makes them feel like they are building an impressive resume and if they don't have time to finish their work, they can point to their busy schedule for sympathy. Busy Bodies may be filling the hours in their days, but they are often scattered, and use their time inefficiently. Let me tell you about a Busy Body I knew.

Amanda (Names have been changed to protect….the guilty?)

Amanda was a Busy Body that I knew in college. She was in every activity imaginable and I mean EVERY activity. Marching band, Ultimate Frisbee, Young Democrats, dance, her sorority…you name it. If it was a club on campus, Amanda had probably been involved with it at some point or another. I sat next to her in one of my general education classes sophomore year and at first was extremely impressed with all she did. "Wow, this girl must be a talented superhuman!" I actually felt guilty for not being involved in more things myself. The more I got to know her, however, the more that impression changed.

It started when Amanda missed a class one day and asked me if she'd missed anything. She told me she'd had an extra dance practice and couldn't make it. I gave her the notes and didn't think much of it…until it happened again…and again. Amanda began missing class all the time, each time with an excuse more dramatic than before:

"I've been so busy with swimming lately, you wouldn't believe it!"

"This dance show next week has me so busy I can't think straight!"

"I couldn't come to class because I stayed up all night last night writing a paper that I'd been too busy to do earlier!"

I quickly became frustrated that I was coming to class and putting in the time, but Amanda was getting all the notes from me for nothing. I guess part of me felt a little abused, but it was hard for me to say no so we continued to skate through the semester this way until…

One night my friends and I decided to go see the midnight showing of a new movie. You know, the kind of thing where you have to get there super early to get in line for tickets. (A bit nerdy, I'll admit, but a ton of fun!) Guess who showed up right before us in line? Amanda. Amanda who is far too busy to come to class, but has five hours to camp out for movie tickets. Her days of getting free notes from me ended right then and there.

Don't be an Amanda

Amanda's problem was that she saw many opportunities in college and wanted to seize every single one of them. She thought that by jam-packing her days with activities, she was putting herself on a path to success, but she wasn't able to manage all of these obligations effectively. The worst

> ❖It's not only college students who use the "I'm too busy" excuse! I've heard everyone from elementary school students to teachers use this line.

part is that when she needed an excuse, she told people, "I'm too busy." There are two problems with that excuse.

1) We all have busy lives. Some of us just manage our time better than others.
2) Being "busy" only fills time. Being productive moves toward a goal and is far more valuable.

We've all used the "I'm too busy" line at some point or another but I urge you to drop it from your vocabulary.

Where Does the Busy Body Come From?

There may be some justification to why this Busy Body attitude is so common. Our society is obsessed with linking the words "busy" and "important" even though they don't necessarily have anything to do with each other. When I first met Amanda, I was jealous of all the activities she did and felt as though I wasn't involved enough. I didn't base this feeling off of any of her productive accomplishments, only her busy schedule. How silly!

If you think about it, we've all been trained to think that "busy" is something to strive for since we first started high school. Remember what your guidance counselors encouraged you to do? Join a club! Get involved in an activity! Build that resume! The star students were the ones who not only took the honors classes, but also participated in band, cheerleading, sports, volunteer work, after school clubs, underwater basket weaving, you name it! What did your parents tell you to do if they caught you sitting around doing nothing? Get up and do something! Stop being lazy and go pick up a hobby, do your homework, clean your room! We become trained at a young age to think busy people are successful people and so we naturally want to proudly proclaim how incredibly busy we are as we get older.

We Make Time for What's Important

> **Top 5 Excuses to Never Tell Your Professor:**
>
> **1) I've been too busy** *Your professors are busier than you can imagine.*
>
> **2) My computer broke** *There are computers in the library. Keep trying.*
>
> **3) My <insert elderly relative> died** *Unless this line is actually true, Granny doesn't appreciate being lied about.*
>
> **4) I had an important University event last night** *And what about all the other nights?*
>
> **5) I didn't understand the assignment** *Then you should have asked.*

I'm not saying being involved is bad. No! It's important to be well-rounded and to stay involved in things you care about. However, make sure these activities are productive and not just filling your time. When you use "I'm too busy" as an excuse for not getting your work done, your professors and your classmates will have no sympathy for you. Remember, they have lives too! When you say you're "too busy" what you're really saying is that you've decided to use your time for things that you think are more important. We all make time for what's important to us.

The bottom line, is that in order to mange your time effectively in college, you need to focus on quality not quantity. Busy bodies focus on the quantity of things they do. Successful students focus on the quality and productivity of what they do.

Is What I'm Doing Worth It?

So how do you know if the activities in your schedule are making the best use of your time? Sometimes when students really take an honest look at the things they are doing, they realize that some activities aren't as beneficial as they may seem. Those kinds of things are like extra "fat" in your schedule you need to get rid of. Carefully consider any activities you may be involved in because they sound better than they actually are.

I'll be completely honest with you, in high school, I joined "Girl's League" just because all my friends were in it and I thought that's what smart girls at my school were supposed to do. It didn't interest me and I never contributed anything to the club other than my presence, but I thought it made me look smart. When I went to fill out my college applications, I didn't even include it on my resume because I was afraid someone would ask me what I did in that club and I wouldn't have a good answer. How dumb is that? I wish I could have back all those wasted lunch periods.

Think about all the things you are involved in, including class, clubs or jobs and use them to fill out the following chart.

Thing I Do	Amount of Time it Takes	What I Gain from it	Worth it? (Yes or No)
1)			
2)			
3)			
4)			
5)			

Look over the chart you just made. If the amount of time you're putting into something is not worth what you are getting out of it, then why are you doing it? The great thing about college is that you have more control over what you do than you ever have before.

Stop the Comparison

As you're looking over your chart, make sure you don't let your perceptions of other peoples' schedules sway your decisions. Just because an activity is popular or all of your friends are doing it doesn't mean it's the right use of your time. Everyone has different goals and you need to pick activities that contribute to your goals, not someone else's.

Over-Committing Yourself

So what happens if all the things you're doing are really important and all end up being "worth it" in your chart, but you still feel like you're drowning in work? Well, first of all, I want to recommend that you don't think of yourself as "over-committed" until you've finished this book and start implementing

> ◆ Being involved in many things isn't worth it if you can't keep up with the schedule.

some of the strategies in The Time Diet. You need to analyze whether you're stressed because you actually do not have enough hours in the day, or because you're not managing your time well enough as precious hours go by unused. You are capable of more than you think.

That being said, even with the best time management skills it is possible to take on more than you can physically handle and college is not the time for a nervous breakdown! College presents so many exciting new opportunities, but we all have our limits. If you've made significant improvements to your time management skills and you still feel like your work is severely impacting your emotional health and quality of life, something needs to go. In this case, the chart above isn't about which things you're doing are "worth it" but rather which things are the *least* worth it.

Managing a Rigorous Academic Schedule

If you feel as though your academic load alone, rather than the addition of extra curriculum activities, is what has you overwhelmed, it is time to look at your class schedule. Can you put off taking a class until a different semester? It may mean paying more money down the line, but what price do you put on your sanity? Before you register for classes next semester, talk to other students in your degree program who are a year or two ahead of you. They usually have a pretty good idea about the workload and stress level that various required classes entail. If you can avoid taking two incredibly stressful classes in the same semester, do it! Make sure to plan ahead and register for classes as soon as they become available. This way, you'll have the most flexibility with choosing a schedule that works for you. There is nothing worse than planning out the perfect schedule only to discover that all of those classes are now full.

Time-Based vs. Accomplishment-Based Breaks

When you sit down for a productive afternoon of homework, you'll eventually need to take a break. However, how you decide when to take breaks from your work can reveal a lot about whether you value being busy or being productive. I'm sure you've heard that it's a good idea to force yourself to work for a set period of time and then reward yourself with a break. One of my teachers used to tell us to work for 50 minutes and then give ourselves the last ten minutes of that hour as a break. This is what I call a "time-based reward." While sometimes these are necessary, time-based rewards emphasize quantity over quality and reward being busy instead of being productive.

Consider this: You're writing a paper and have told yourself you'll work on it for half an hour and then give yourself a break. As soon as you start your work, you're watching that clock tick down minute-by-minute until you get to stop working. Once 30 of those minutes have ticked by, you've "earned" your break whether you've written two pages or two sentences. Time-based rewards reward the passage of time, not the accomplishment of a task.

No one would go on a diet like that. When people go on a diet, they often have an end goal in mind. "I want to lose ten pounds," they might say. Few people will tell you, "I'm going to eat healthy for five days and then I'll be happy." The objective of a diet is not simply to let time pass, it's to work toward a goal.

The same is true for your Time Diet. Using "accomplishment-based rewards" puts the emphasis on achieving specific accomplishments rather than just letting time pass. When writing a paper, instead of giving yourself a break after 30 minutes of work why not promise yourself a break when you have completed your first page? If that only takes you

> ◈ I urge you to give accomplishment-based breaks a try. If your old way of doing things still works better, great! But remember: it's important to frequently re-evaluate your work habits to make sure they are still the best choice for you.

ten minutes, great! You get your break sooner! Now you actually have motivation to get a set chunk of work done instead of waiting for a set amount of time to pass. Don't be afraid to make your goal too small either! If you know this particular paper is going to be very difficult for you, make your initial goal be to write the first paragraph. You'll feel much more deserving of your break if you know you've earned it.

But wait! What if I only have a short amount of time to devote to a task? How can I take accomplishment-based breaks when there is only a brief block of time to work on something? The goal I set for myself will probably take longer than the time I actually have! Don't worry. Yes, accomplishment-based breaks work best when you have an extended period of available time in front of you, but that doesn't mean you can't also use them when you only have a half an hour to spare. Let's say you just got back to your dorm from the campus recreation center. After a quick shower, you now only have 30 minutes before you have to leave to meet a friend for dinner, but you really want to get a jump-start on your language translation project. It wouldn't really be fair to your friend in this case to use accomplishment-based breaks. (You could tell yourself you'll go meet your friend after you finish two pages of translation, but that could take an hour!) Instead, set a timer or an alarm to go off in 30 minutes and *do not look at the clock*! This way, you can completely focus on the task at hand without being tempted to watch each minute tick by. You're now thinking more about your work than the passage of time.

Redefining Breaks

To make the most of accomplishment-based rewards, you might have to re-think what a "break" is. Many times people think of a break as some sort of Dessert. It is an enjoyable thing that takes your mind off of work for a while. This is true, but if you start breaking your tasks into smaller and smaller chunks to make them more manageable, you may find yourself spending more time taking Dessert rewards than completing Meat and Vegetable work! Think about making rewards really small things. For example, you could decide that every time you finish a page of your paper, you will allow yourself to check Facebook for a few minutes (just keep it short!) These little "mini breaks" still give you something to look forward to and because they are so short, you can take more of them.

Also, it is important to remember that a break doesn't always have to be a Dessert task during which you stop working. A break can be anything that gives your mind a rest. This is where those really mindless Vegetable tasks come in handy! When I was in college,

> ◆ Choosing to fold laundry (or some other mindless chore) as a break from something more difficult will cause you to actually look forward to folding laundry. How crazy is that?!

one of my favorite mindless breaks was to fold laundry. I was still doing something that needed to be done, but it took no brainpower whatsoever. I didn't have to think about anything other than which socks went together or deciding which shirts got folded and which ones I hung up. Some other examples of mindless break tasks are

1) Changing your sheets and towels
2) Putting books and papers away
3) Vacuuming your room
4) Cleaning out your desk drawer
5) Backing up your computer

Now, think of a few other mindless tasks to add to this list.

6)

7)

8)

9)

10)

Remember, it is still very important to take breaks from work and do Dessert things that you enjoy, but it's easier to find the motivation to do mindless tasks (like laundry) when you view them as a break from more difficult work, rather than something annoying that you have to do.

Never Underestimate the Power of a Nap

One of my favorite ways to reward accomplishments is with a nap! This is especially true when I wake up early to finish work and am getting sleepy by mid-afternoon. Be careful that you plan these naps carefully however! A nap is not the kind of reward you want to give yourself after writing one paragraph. This is a more heavy-duty kind of reward that you save for after you've accomplished something big, or when you're really stressed and you need to completely shut down for a few minutes. Naps can re-energize you and allow your brain to re-charge. Never take naps for longer than half an hour and don't take them too close to bedtime. If you nap for longer than half an hour, you run the risk of it doing more harm than good. Have you ever woken up from a nap feeling groggy, disoriented and confused? You probably slept too long. A nap that lasts too long leaves you feeling frustrated because it's longer than you needed to re-charge, but shorter than you needed for that refreshed feeling of a good night's sleep. Set your alarm for 20-30 minutes and then wake up and move on with your day.

Breaking up Meat Tasks

Remember, accomplishment-based rewards serve two purposes. They encourage you to be productive rather than merely "busy," and they also break up large Meat tasks into more manageable and less daunting bits. An author friend of mine told me that when she is writing a book, her goal is to write five pages a day. Some days that takes her an hour, some days it takes her three, but after writing those five pages, she doesn't have to touch the book again that day if she doesn't feel like it. Writing a book is a huge Meat

> ◆Saving all the difficult tasks for later may seem like a good idea at the time, but remember, later always gets here eventually!

task — it takes a lot of time and a lot of thinking. Breaking it down into little five-page chunks makes accomplishing this Meat task a lot less stressful and much more manageable.

When we don't break up large Meat tasks into chunks, here is what tends to happen. We work on something until it becomes difficult, and then we move on to something else. This works for a little while until we have done all the easy parts and we are only left with the difficult parts. No wonder you are so unmotivated to work! Let's say that your homework for the week was to:

-Read two chapters and be prepared for a class discussion
-Finish a worksheet of five math problems that may or may not be collected at the beginning of class
-Read one chapter for another class that won't be tested until the midterm
-Post a brief reflection on the class blog site about your reading

If you tackle this randomly, you are likely to complete all the easy parts first, and then be stuck with only difficult things. This is what could happen:

-Read one chapter and then get a little confused and choose to save the rest for "later."
-Finish three of the five math problems, and then get stuck and decide to put off the other two.
-Get a few paragraphs into the reading, realize it is insanely dense, and just cross your fingers that it'll make more sense to you before the midterm.
-You finish the reading for your blog post, but know that summarizing it is going to be next to impossible so you put it off.

The next day, when you sit down to work, your options are pretty bleak. Your choices are:

1) Finish some dense reading
2) Finish two difficult math problems or
3) Summarize some reading that simply can't be summed up in any less than two pages.

No wonder you are having a hard time motivating yourself to sit down and work! You left yourself with only difficult things to do! Now you're more tempted to just not finish the work and cross your fingers that the professor doesn't collect the homework or won't call on you to give your opinion on the reading.

Instead, you could have broken up all the work into manageable chunks and tackled one chunk a day. Take the math problems for example. If you told yourself you were going to do only a few problems a day, then one day it might have taken ten minutes and one day it would have taken 45, but you have spread out the difficulty so you're not saving all the tough ones for the end.

It's All About Control

If you start to become overwhelmed with your schedule, it's important to remember that you have control over all of it. Now, you may be thinking, "Control? I certainly don't feel like I have any control. It's not like I'm choosing to do all this homework!!"

This brings us to Myth #2:

Myth #2: Your Schedule Controls You

Most high school seniors are very anxious to get to college. "Woohoo!" they say. "I'm done with my mandatory K-12 education! Starting now, I'm doing things for me! I don't have to listen to my parents anymore! I'm an adult!" Then they get to college and

> ◆Nobody controls you except YOU! Embrace the power and use it responsibly.

realize that instead of listening to their parents, they are now listening to their professors and their deadlines. These professors may not be telling them to clean their room like their parents always did at home, but they *are* telling them to study, work hard and turn in homework on time.

While it's true that you do have far more freedom in college, it is easy to think that by trying to get good grades in college, you won't be able to have any fun. Movies and television certainly do their best to perpetuate this myth. How many movies about college have you seen in which the "smart" student who gets good grades wasn't some nerd with giant glasses who never leaves the dorm room to actually see the light of day? Not too many, and that's a shame. That isn't what real life is like.

All of the freedom in college comes with another wonderful thing: control. Guess what, your professor is not in control of your time, you are. Remember, we make time for what's important to us. If getting good grades and having fun are both important to you, you have to make time for both. You control how many social activities you put onto your calendar, and giving up the occasional party to study for a midterm does not mean you have "no fun." It means you're smart about your time.

Everything you do each day is completely your choice. There is no "Schedule Fairy" who forces you to do anything. "Choosing" to do something puts you in control while "having" to do something doesn't. We all have 1,440 minutes in every day, and as each one ticks by, you choose how to spend it.

I know you've heard the whole "we all have the same number of hours in the day" speech before. Well, it's famous because it's true. It's easy to try to blame other people for your own lack of interest in meeting a deadline, but in reality, when you're on your Time Diet, you are in complete control of how you organize yourself. Think about a regular diet. If you're trying to give up carbs, who has the ultimate say over whether or not you shove that ooey, gooey, piece of delicious garlic bread into your mouth? You do. The same is true for The Time Diet. Your friends may beg you to go out instead of doing your homework, or the rainy weather may be telling you to skip class and take a nap instead, but things like that don't control you. Only you control you.

Procrastination: Giving up Control

The problem, of course, is that many college students procrastinate. Waiting until the last minute to do things means giving up the control you once had over your schedule. For instance, let's say a professor gives you a week to write a paper. At the beginning of that week, you have complete control over when you write it. You can do it Monday night, Wednesday morning or maybe even on sunny Thursday afternoon as you sit outside on a blanket on the quad. You can record your favorite show or watch it later on Hulu to make sure your paper takes priority of your "primetime" hours. You can go to the library where you know it will be quiet and you'll be able to concentrate instead of sitting in the lounge of your dorm and talking with friends. There are endless ways you can rearrange your schedule to get that paper done.

> ◆Procrastination is the enemy of time management. Don't put things off until "later" because "later" quickly becomes "now."

However, as the deadline gets closer and closer you have less and less control over when you do the paper. Finally, at midnight on the night before this paper is due, you are at the mercy of the deadline. You have now given up all the control you once had and have given it to the deadline instead. Now the paper is due in eight hours! You no longer have a choice about when you do it. The deadline says you must do it NOW.

Why Do We Procrastinate?

The best way to stop putting things off is to figure out why we love procrastinating in the first place. There are four mains reasons college students procrastinate.

1) They don't like the work they have to do
2) They don't know where to start
3) They work better up against a deadline
4) They are afraid of failure

"I Don't Want To!"

The most common reason we procrastinate is because sometimes, we just really *really* don't want to do our homework. We know we should work, but work isn't fun and watching college sports and reality T.V. is. Don't worry. You're not alone. Even the best students feel like this sometimes. Here are some ways to motivate yourself to do homework you just don't want to do.

Break a large project into smaller pieces.
The best way to combat laziness is to break up a Meat task into smaller pieces and tackle them one piece at a time. For example, if you have a research paper to write, you may not want to start it because it seems like such an immense task that you don't have the energy to tackle. Watching TV, going to the gym or getting a root canal all sound more appealing than starting something so overwhelming. Instead, break the large project into smaller chunks that are more manageable. Instead of saying "I'm going to start my research paper today" say, "I am going to start my research paper today by compiling a bibliography of library sources." Setting smaller daily goals makes a large project feel more approachable.

Promise yourself a reward.
We can all agree, there are a ton of things in life that are more fun than doing hard work! Instead of having the mindset that your work is preventing you from doing something fun, just re-frame your thinking. You are still going to both have fun and get work done today, but you are just going to switch the order around a little bit. When you finish compiling your bibliography for your research paper, then you are going to reward yourself with a 10-minute chill-out session with your iPod, or run over to the Student Center for a smoothie.

Be creative with your rewards. Rewarding yourself with a lengthy break or Dessert task every time you finish a difficult chunk of work is not always practical. Instead, be creative with your rewards, particularly if you are trying to save money and a java mocha chiller just isn't in the budget every time you need a pat on the back. A reward can be as simple as stepping outside for some fresh air, eating a few jellybeans from your drawer stash, or texting with a friend.

Finally, remember that putting off your homework won't make it go away even though you really wish it would!

Searching for an Idea

Another common reason that college students procrastinate is because they have a big project to tackle and they don't really know where to start. We want to work, we just haven't come up with the perfect project idea yet. We wait and wait, hoping the perfect idea will come to us. Pretty soon, the due date is tomorrow and we haven't even started! Don't let this happen to you!

Give Yourself Thinking Time

You can't just wait around hoping an idea will come to you. Sometimes you need to give it a little help. You need to purposefully clear your mind and give yourself some time to think. There is a reason people come up with brilliant ideas in the shower. Their mind is clear and they are not focused on doing anything else.

Change Your Scenery

Sometimes just working in a different place can be enough of a change to get the creative juices flowing. If you always work at your desk, try sitting at a coffee shop. If you always work in the library, try sitting outside. When you are surrounded by new things you're more likely to think of new things too.

Just Start Working

The truth of the matter is, we can wait a lifetime for the perfect idea to come to us. At some point, we need to just start working! If you don't have the perfect idea yet, just take the best one you have and start going with it. It's easier to edit your work later than to keep staring at that intimidating blank screen on your computer! Sometimes it's more important to get it done than to try to get it done perfectly on the first try.

Creating Your Own Deadlines

Many college students often justify procrastination by saying they work better when they are up against the pressure of a deadline. I don't happen to work that way, but I had many friends in college who did. Let's take a typical college student (who we will call "Ryan") as an example. Ryan purposefully procrastinates because he finds it difficult to focus until he's got the pressure of a deadline looming.

Ryan has a paper assigned to him on Monday that is due the following Monday. But, true to form, he has waited until Sunday evening to start the paper. Instead of having a week to write it, he has only a few hours. The good news is that Ryan is now forced to tune out all distractions and provide nothing but focused work. The bad news is that he now has to hope no unexpected crisis or distraction comes up that will prevent him from writing this paper—no power outages, no 24-hour stomach bug, no girlfriend dramas. He also will probably be up until 2:00a.m. and will therefore be tired and cranky the next day. Wouldn't it be cool if Ryan could have drawn on that same kind of focused work without having to wait until the last minute?

The way to do this is to create your own deadline before the actual deadline occurs. Tell your roommate/friend/family member about your deadline and ask them to check on you. Now you are accountable to not only yourself, but to someone else as well. Instead of thinking of Monday as

> ◈While you're still getting used to sticking to self-made deadlines, get your friends involved. Tell a trusted friend about your deadline and encourage them to check up on you. You just can't get mad at them for nagging!

his deadline, Ryan could have told himself his paper was actually due on Thursday. To force himself to stick to his deadline, he could have also made plans with his roommate to go out on Friday night if his paper were done. This way, he would now be accountable to his roommate for his self-made deadline. If something unexpected came up and he wasn't able to get his work done by Thursday, he would still have the weekend to fall back on.

Combating Fear of Failure

The final reason college students put off their work is because they are afraid of not doing it well enough. This is particularly common among over-achieving students who were at the top of their classes in high school, but now find themselves to be "average" compared to their equally highly-achieving peers. If you catch yourself procrastinating on a task because of a fear of failure, ask yourself the following question:

Whose expectations am I afraid I won't meet?

It is helpful to isolate exactly who you are afraid of not impressing.

> ◈Sometimes it's hard to admit that we're afraid of failing. It's OK. Everyone has felt it at some point or another.

If that person is your professor...make a mental list of all the times you have succeeded for him or her. Think of all the times you've answered a question correctly

29

in class, or done well on a homework assignment. Why would this time be any different? Picture yourself telling your professor that you didn't get this project done on time because you were afraid he or she wouldn't think it was good enough. What do you envision the reaction to be? Any teacher would much rather see work completed, even if it isn't perfect, than not done at all.

If that person is a friend or group of friends...ask yourself why you are working so hard to impress people who like you anyway? Sometimes, people worry about maintaining an image for those around them, particularly if that image is "the smart one." Being "the smart one" in the class may have come very easily in high school, but students often find that in a community of college peers, the competition is steeper. Relax! I promise your friends won't think any less of you if you get a B on a project, but you'll look pretty dumb if you just don't turn it in!

Often, the person you are actually afraid of disappointing is yourself. This is most commonly a problem for perfectionists or for people who have been told their whole lives how smart they are or how much potential they have. That is a lot to live up to! Remember that not everything you do has to be perfect. Part of being successful is trying, failing, reevaluating and then trying again. Fear of failure is one of the biggest hurdles of success.

Beware of Pollyannas

Pollyannas are those chirpy friends that encourage you to procrastinate. We've all experienced a Pollyanna before. He or she usually shows up right before you have a major project to do. They are the kind of friends who put their arm around you and say, "You worry too much! It'll all get done! Let's go out for ice cream." That's easy for them to say because you are the one who actually has to do the work! The Pollyanna attitude causes you to think that things just "happen" or take far less time than they actually do. This attitude is dangerous because when the reality of the deadline finally hits, you may have run out of time and risk getting a "zero" on your work.

Brittany

I worked part-time as an undergrad and one of my co-workers was a Pollyanna. We weren't great friends, but got to know each other as well as people do when they work beside each other every other day. When Brittany would hear me say no to a social engagement because of homework, I would always hear the same speech: "You know, life is about having fun! Don't worry about your studying, it'll get done! Go out and party!"

Needless to say, Brittany was always up all night in the library the night before a major assignment was due. Even if she hadn't told me about these late night cram-sessions, it wasn't too difficult to tell that's what was going on. She would show up to work the next day with a giant cup of coffee, bags under her eyes and wearing the same clothes as she did the day before. I guess she didn't end up passing all of those classes either because Brittany didn't graduate when I did. In fact, she ended up graduating as a 6th year senior. She may have thought she had more fun in college than I did, but she's wrong. I had a wonderful time as an undergrad and also thoroughly enjoyed actually getting a full night of rest before Finals. Also, I graduated two years ahead of Brittany and was able to get a real job with a real paycheck that much quicker. It's amazing how much more fun a little extra money in your pocket can buy!

Optimism Isn't Bad

There is a difference between being a realistic and an un-realistic optimist. Pollyannas encourage an unrealistic optimism. They make you think things just happen without having any kind of plan for *how* they will happen. This is why people under the spell of a

> ◆ When Pollyannas try to convince you to procrastinate, just remember: it isn't *their* work they want you to put off, it's *yours.*

Pollyanna don't usually get much done and often don't appreciate the huge amount of work that goes into actually completing a complex task. The realistic optimist on the other hand knows exactly what it will take to complete a task and has the confidence that it can be done.

Being a Realistic Optimist

It is easy to turn the "Pollyanna attitude" into a realistic optimist attitude. Whenever you catch yourself saying, "Oh, it'll all get done," ask yourself, "How?" Being sure of the "how" will lead you to turn Pollyanna-ish statements into realistic ones. For example:

"I won't worry about this now, it'll all get done somehow."

becomes…

"It'll all get done because I have set aside 1:00p.m.-2:00p.m. each day over the next few days to get it done and I have great confidence in my persistence and motivation to get it done. Nothing will stand in my way!"

Now you're starting to sound like a realistic optimist!

Silence Your Inner Time Waster

Learning to tune out people who try to convince you to procrastinate is one thing. Learning to silence that inner voice of your own that tells you to procrastinate can be much harder. That is because we all have that little voice inside us that hates doing work. It's that voice that creeps out when you're just about to start some work that says, "Why work now? Look at that big wonderful television! You know you want to watch that new reality show. Just watch it! When you're done you're bound to feel much more like working!" In a regular diet you might recognize this as the same voice that tells you that it's ok to eat that second piece of chocolate cake because you've "earned" it, or to grab a slice of pizza for lunch instead of making yourself a sandwich because it's easier. This is your Inner Time Waster and you need to learn to shut it up.

> ### Top 3 Excuses your Inner Time Waster tells you
>
> **1) None of your friends are working right now.** *Of course it seems like your friends never work. You usually hang out with them when you're having fun, not working, right?*
>
> **2) You deserve a break, do it later!** *You do deserve a break, and that's why you're going to take one…right after you actually accomplish something.*
>
> **3) You'll feel more like working later.** *No you won't. You'll feel like having fun later. So, get your work out of the way and enjoy the rest of your time!*

Your Inner Time Waster can be extremely convincing. It is very good at finding any possible reason to put off doing your work. Sometimes it'll try to tell you that you'll feel more like doing work later, or that you work all the time and deserve a break. It's particularly good at convincing you to put off easy tasks that should only take a few minutes until the infamous "later." Do not be fooled. Do you really think you'll feel more like working later? No. This rarely happens. Get started now so you have less to do when "later" gets here.

Don't let your Inner Time Waster take control of you. You're choosing to get your work done first so that you can enjoy your free time later. You're already scheduling Desserts for yourself so you have no excuse to put off work. Tell your Inner Time Waster to get lost!

The "Choose-To" List

Because all of our daily tasks are ultimately choices we control and not things we are forced to do, the "to-do" list will hereby be referred to as the "Choose-To" List. I really don't like being told to do something. I'd much rather choose to do it.

I know what you're thinking. "I don't *choose* to take a final, and to pay my rent, and to go to my job. I *have* to do all of those things and I don't like it!" Wrong. You take a final because you recognize the importance of a college education and you know that in order to get the job you want, you need a degree. Therefore you need this class

> ❖Embracing the Choose-To List is an essential part of perfecting your attitude about time management. With a "to-do" list, tasks have the control. With a Choose-To List, YOU have the control. That's what The Time Diet is all about.

and need to take this final to pass it. You pay rent because having a place to call your own is important to you. You could stop paying, get evicted and try to get by on couch-surfing with your friends. That would be the consequence of that choice. You can only avoid that consequence by choosing to continue paying rent.

I hate washing dishes. I hated it while I was living at home, I hated it while I lived in my college apartment and I hate it now in my own house. I have contemplated many times what would happen if I simply stopped washing them. They would probably pile up for a while in the sink. When the sink got full, they would pile up on the counter. When the counter got full, I would probably run out of dishes, so I would have to buy paper ones instead. This would get expensive and messy. While I don't like washing dishes, the thought of eating off paper plates my whole life makes me feel like a bit of a loser, so I continue to scrub off my plate at the end of every meal. Not because I have to, because I choose to.

There Are No "Have-Tos" Only "Choose-Tos."

The difference between "choosing" to do something rather than "having" to do something may seem insignificant at first. After all, you are still probably going to dread doing the task. However, the key to effective time management is not necessarily enjoying every task you do, but feeling in control of everything you do. The sooner you begin to view your to-do list as choices instead of mandates, the sooner you will feel in control of your own day.

The following worksheet will help you take control of your day.

Consider the tasks you do on a regular basis that you truly hate doing. Now, imagine never doing them again and consider what the results would be. I'll give you a few examples to get you started.

Task I hate	What would happen if I didn't do it?
1) **Studying for my final**	*I would probably fail the class and not graduate when I'm supposed to.*
2) **Exercising**	*The "Freshmen 15" could become the "Freshmen 20 or 25"*
3)	
4)	
5)	
6)	
7)	

Now, consider your answers in the right columns. Are these scenarios worth it to you? The answer doesn't always have to be "no." Sometimes the implications of Column Two are life changing ("I would flunk out of school" or "I wouldn't have a place to live") but they are not always so dire. Let's look at the laundry scenario. Most college students hate doing laundry. You have to wait around to put the clothes in the dryer, you have to find enough quarters to stick in the stupid machine and you always realize you're out of clothes at the least convenient time. So, you hate doing laundry? Go ahead, stop doing it! You probably won't notice a difference for the first few weeks, but then, you'll be completely out of clothes. You'll start re-wearing all of your clothes again....and again. By the third time through your wardrobe, you're probably going to really start to smell. Then, you have two options: you can continue to gross out everyone around you and embrace the fact that at least now you'll have a three-seat buffer of personal space (in all directions) in class, or you can spend money you probably don't have to go buy more clothes. That second option will get really expensive after a while.

Now that you've examined what will happen if you stop doing laundry, you can weigh whether or not the consequences of not doing it are worth the benefits. For me personally, I value my dignity too much to offend my peers by smelling really bad and I also don't have the money to buy a new wardrobe every month. If you do have that kind of money, and you hate doing laundry that much, then go for it. I envy you. For the rest of you, suck it up and do your laundry. You're choosing to do it because you want the desired outcome and to have control of your life.

Motivation Management

At this point, I realize you may want to throw this book across the room. "OK great, so I'm choosing to do all these boring things in my life, but I still don't want to! How do I make myself want to?"

I'm going to let you in on a little secret: People who have great time management skills and always get work done by the deadline don't always want to do everything they do either, but they do it anyway! Do you think people on a low-fat diet really love eating fruits and veggies all the time and wouldn't love to chow down on French fries and jelly donuts? People on a Time Diet know that sometimes getting work done can be a pain, but it's worth it. It's all about having self-control and motivation.

This is why the phrase "time management" can be somewhat of a misnomer. Very often we know we have the time to do something but we just can't find the motivation to actually do it. Instead of starting our task, we end up putting it off, hoping we'll feel more like doing it later. This is an issue of motivation management. There are really two ways to manage your motivation. The first way is to maximize the time you do feel motivated and the second is to manufacture inspiration when it won't come naturally.

Maximizing Motivation

If you're actually motivated to do something you will do a better job in a faster amount of time. That is good news for your Time Diet! If you're choosing between several tasks to do, you're sometimes better off choosing the one you're more motivated to do, even if something else is due sooner. This of course doesn't apply to things that you're always motivated to do. For example, I had a friend in college who loved doing her math homework because she was really good at it and it made her feel smart. She didn't need to worry about being motivated to do her math homework because she

◆This may sound obvious, but avoid classes you truly have no interest in whenever possible. Your major may require specific courses, but you generally have more freedom with your General Education courses. Do your research and ask around about what different G.E.s are really like before signing up. It may be worth it to wait for a different semester when a class that really interests you is offered.

always was. However, let's say that you, like me, hate doing reading for classes that don't interest you in the first place. As an undergrad, I took a class on earthquakes to fulfill a General Education requirement and it was seriously the most boring class in the world. I never wanted to do any work for it. Then, one day I was reminiscing with my mom about the big Whittier, California earthquake years ago and I suddenly wanted to learn more about earthquakes.

Wow! I never wanted to do work for this class and now I suddenly did. I needed to take advantage of it right away! I sat down and did my reading for that week and started my lab report that was supposed to serve as our final in that class. Was it my most pressing deadline at the moment? No. But I knew I needed to maximize my new-found (and sadly, temporary) motivation.

Finding Inspiration

We all know that inspiration is sometimes hard to come by. Usually, we have to dig around for motivation to complete a task. So how do you do that? You might have to get a little creative. One of my favorite ways to find inspiration for undesirable homework is with a change of scenery. Don't want to do that statistics homework? Maybe you'll be more inclined to do it if you can at least sit outside and enjoy the warmth and sunshine of a beautiful day! If outside isn't an option, try going to a coffee shop, a funky café, the library, or even just a different part of your dorm or apartment. Teachers will commonly turn all their students' desks around to face another wall to get a more focused learning day. Why does that work? Because it's a change of scenery. Being surrounded by different things may be just enough stimulation to break up the monotony of work and get you motivated to keep going.

Some college students try to break the monotony by doing homework with a friend or classmate. Unless this is a group project, I don't recommend this strategy unless you're absolutely 100% sure that you will actually get the work done. Usually studying with a friend takes twice as long to complete because you distract each other. I'd rather get my work done in half the time and then go out and enjoy my friend's company.

Visualization

Visualization can be another great tool to help you find motivation. Exercise class instructors use this technique all the time. They'll say things like, "Come on! Let's move! Think how great you'll look in that swim suit this summer." Or "Think about how great your arms will look with that awesome muscle definition!" Why do you think they say these things, especially during really difficult points in the

> ◆Visualization only works as a motivation tool if you let yourself get into it a little bit. It's more than just thinking, "Oh, wouldn't it be nice if I had more work done?" You actually have to vividly imagine a weight being lifted from your shoulders when your work is done. It works for me every time.

workout? Because visualizing a desired result helps us find the will to do undesirable things. When you are doing school work that you really don't want to do, and you catch yourself thinking, "Maybe I'll stop now and do the rest later," visualize what you'll feel like when the homework is all done. Picture yourself crawling into bed that night being completely worry-free because that assignment is finished. If you keep working at it for a little bit longer, that vision could be reality!

Review

OK, you're doing great so far! Let's review what we learned in this section:

1) There are three types of tasks: Meats, Vegetables and Desserts. You need a good balance of all three to maintain a healthy Time Diet.

2) Busy does not equal productive. Don't be a Busy-Body who uses the "I'm too busy" excuse to not do something. We make time for what's important to us.

3) Your schedule does not control you. You can be a good student and still have fun by setting your own deadlines that work around your social schedule.

4) When you procrastinate, you give up the control you once had over your time.

5) There are no "have tos" only "choose-tos." Even if you don't enjoy doing your homework, you can rejoice in the fact that you are choosing to do it.

Most importantly, remember that having the right attitude is essential to a successful Time Diet. Time management is not something you "do." Rather, it's the way you look at your schedule. You're not going to love every single thing you do. The trick is to have the self-discipline to do it anyway because you know it's worth it.

PART 2
THE NUTS AND BOLTS OF ORGANIZATION

Emily Schwartz

You are making great progress on your Time Diet so far! You know how to categorize all the things you do during the day into the three "time food groups": Meats, Vegetables and Desserts. You know that you, not your professors, your friends or anyone else, have control over your time and that the only way you give up that control is by procrastinating. You recognize that sometimes you may be less than thrilled to finish your work, but you're learning to be a master self-motivator.

You're now prepared to move on to the next step of your college Time Diet. The first part of this book was all about changing the way you think about time management. This section is all about how to take this new way of thinking and use it to better organize your day. Now, I know some of you read that last sentence, saw the word "organize" and thought to yourself, "Well, it's been a nice book so far, but I'm not an organized person so this part will never help me."

That brings us to Myth #3:

Myth #3: The Color Coded Calendar is the Only Way

When people think of organized time management, the super-detailed color-coded calendar often comes to mind. Have you ever seen something like this? I had a friend in college who took the color-coded calendar to new heights. She used gel pens in every color imaginable and each one had a purpose. Reading assignments were written in purple, band practice was in red, football games were in green, quizzes were in burnt orange and study sessions were written in aquamarine. Every minute of every day was carefully scripted out in handwriting so perfect, it would make your old fourth grade teacher salivate. Her calendar was a quite a sight to behold.

It's easy to think *that* is what it means to be organized. People who aren't that neat and obsessive simply don't have a hope at organizing their life so why even try, right? Wrong!

> ◆ If you *want* to have a super-detailed calendar, go ahead! However, you don't *need* that level of detail to have excellent time management skills.

The color-coded calendar is a myth because while it is one way to be organized, it is certainly not the only way. That kind of hyper-organization would never work for me. I would forget what purple and red meant and I would probably lose my aquamarine pen. I can't have every single minute of my life scripted out because it often changes during the day. Have you ever seen people begin a diet and write down every single calorie they consume right down to the last breath mint? Does that work? Sure. But do you really need that level of detail to successfully diet? Or course not, and you don't need it for your Time Diet either. Yes, you do need to have a system to organize your time, but you don't need to have a super-detailed one.

You may think, "I don't need a system of organization. I never kept a calendar or wrote down any of my assignments in high school and I did just fine." Maybe so, but college is different. You need to write things down! In high school, if you didn't show up to class, your parents got a phone call from the attendance office asking where you were. In high school, your schedule was pretty much the same every week. In high school, you still had mom and dad as a safety net if you forgot to do something (as much as you hate to admit.) In college, however, it's all up to you. No one is going to "call home" if you forget to show up to class or a study group. Your professors aren't going to conference with your parents if you don't turn in an assignment. Your parents aren't going to remind you that you have a huge report due on Monday before you try to go out and party on Saturday night.

Not only that, but you have so much more going on in college! You can't possibly expect yourself to remember every little thing on your plate, from that writing assignment due next week to your appointment at your professor's office hours tomorrow to that comedy show coming to campus in a few days. Just write down these things you need to do! Having to write things down is not a "sign of weakness." It doesn't make you any less smart or amazing.

Creating Your System of Organization

So, you may not need a fancy color-coded calendar but you can't just randomly write things down on scraps of paper either. Luckily, you really only need two components to create your own system of organization:

1) A calendar to keep track of long-term deadlines
2) A "Choose-To List" to keep track of daily tasks

These two components can take many forms depending on what works easiest for you, but if you don't have some sort of calendar and some sort of list you'll find time management very difficult!

The Calendar

The calendar is where you keep track of your long-term deadlines, goals and schedules. This is not where you keep track of specific tasks you need to do each day. That's where your Choose-To List comes in. (We'll get to that later.) Your calendar tells you what needs to be accomplished over the span of a week, month or semester. Sometimes students protest that they don't need a calendar because all of their due dates are

> ❖ It's essential to keep all of your deadlines and obligations in one place. This way, you always know exactly where to look to find out what you have coming up!

written down on their course syllabus. True, but you need one central location that contains all of these dates for all of your obligations, not just one class. Besides, your syllabus only tells you the due date for an assignment. In your calendar, you can keep track of not only the due dates for major assignments in all your classes but also the start date you plan to begin working on each of them.

Start Dates and Due Dates

> ❖ It's easy to procrastinate when you tell yourself you'll do an assignment "later." By setting a start date, you tell yourself exactly when "later" is going to be.

A due date is the day an assignment must be completed. If you are only concerned with when something is due, you are far more likely to procrastinate. For example, let's say you have a paper due on April 28th. If you are only concerned with due dates, then the only date associated with this paper in your head will be April 28th. You probably won't even start thinking about that paper until April 28th is very near. By then, you've already allowed a lot of valuable work time to slide and will have a lot to do to complete a paper in a very short amount of time!

This is why students need to also be concerned with start dates. A start date is the day you actually plan to begin an assignment so you'll have enough time to complete it before the due date. If you have a start date planned, you are more likely to spread out your work and far less likely to procrastinate. If you take your same paper that is due on April 28th and set your start date for April 10th, you'll now have that earlier date associated with this assignment. When April 10th is near, you'll know it's time to start your paper and you won't save all of your work until the last minute.

Students' obsession with due dates rather than start dates leads to a stressful problem I like to call "syllabus overload." Syllabus Overload is a highly preventable condition stemming from being overwhelmed with too much to do. Side effects have been known to include panicking, giving up and severe frustration — not to mention a ton of wasted time! Don't let yourself fall victim to this unnecessary waste of your energy. All you need to do is use your calendar correctly.

Syllabus Overload

Syllabus Overload begins on the first day of class on what we all know as "syllabus day." This is when the professor hands out the syllabus (i.e. a schedule of lectures and assignments) and gives the students a quick overview of what they can expect from the class. I have never seen young people listen less to a professor than on syllabus day. While the professor is carefully going through each expectation and assignment, students are madly flipping through the pages looking for words like "term paper" coming anywhere close to the words "minimum 20 pages" or "Final Exam" butting up against the phrase "50% of your grade." Rater than listening, students are trying to quickly assess the stress and workload that will be associated with this particular class.

> ◆A good way to combat Syllabus Overload is to think back to another class you were afraid would be too hard. You got through it right? You'll get through this one too.

When the syllabus part of the class is over and the professor actually tries to teach, no one is listening because they are too busy worrying how they are going to ever get all of this work done and get a good grade. When you multiply this process by four or five (the typical class load for a full time undergrad) in the span of a week, the result can be Syllabus Overload.

True story: When I was in grad school, I once had a really bad case of Syllabus Overload during the first day of a music theory class. If you're not familiar with graduate-level music theory, it involves dissecting every note of a complex classical piece of music and analyzing it according to form and chord structure. I hadn't wanted to take this class, but all the others were full and I needed it in order to graduate. After the first 45 minutes of the class, I was so overwhelmed with all of the huge projects it required, that I spent that rest of that first hour texting my friends to see if they knew of any others classes with space left, and emailing other professors to get on a wait list for their classes. I should not have panicked. Not only did I end up staying in the class, but I also did very well. All of that stress was unnecessary!

How to Cope with Syllabus Overload

Syllabus Overload is a result of students' obsession with due dates rather than start dates. Stressing about all the due dates of a semester instead of planning for when all of this work will be accomplished just wastes time. Instead of allowing yourself to fall into this trap, take your syllabus, grab your calendar and do the following:

1) Look for the "Get to Know You" assignment
Professors often begin the semester with a short assignment that serves as a sort of introduction to what you can expect from the course. Scan your syllabus and find this assignment. Write the due date in your calendar and write "start this assignment" five days before the due date. Do not blow this off because it looks easy! Get started on it as soon as possible and make sure you do your best. You may not think you need five days to finish it, but you certainly don't want this assignment to be late or sloppy. This is the professor's introduction to you and what you are capable of. Do this even for large lecture classes that include breakout sessions with TAs. They will be reading your work from time to time and even grading it. It is very difficult to break a bad first impression.

2) Look for recurring weekly assignments
It is not uncommon for classes to require a weekly reading or writing assignment. This could include posting to an online discussion board, writing a reflection or summary paper, completing a chapter of reading or completing some sort of recurring homework. You should scan the syllabus for these recurring weekly assignments and write in your calendar when you will complete them. Think of these recurring assignments as "Vegetable" tasks. They may not be the most difficult tasks you have to do, but they are still important. It is best to complete these assignments at the same time each week so you know you won't forget about them. For example, if you have Ultimate Frisbee practice on Thursday nights, you can write "post blog

reflection before Frisbee" in your calendar. Also, after the first few weeks you'll have a pretty good idea of how long this assignment takes you to complete and, if need be, you will be able to readjust the time you've allotted for them.

3) Look for major assignments

> ◆Major assignments can be intimidating, especially when you haven't started them yet! You should try to start some small part of a major assignment as soon as you can. It's much easier to finish once you start!

Remember, major assignments are "Meat" tasks and you can't try to tackle them all at once. You need to break them up into smaller chunks and spread them out over time. For papers, look for the suggested page length requirement and its weight on your grade. Write both the due date and the date you plan to start the assignment in your calendar. For papers, a good rule of thumb is to allow at least a day for every three pages you'll need to write. (A "day of work" is defined as a three to four hour chunk of time. If you plan to devote less time than that each day, you'll need to allow more days.) If the paper is heavily research-based, allow one extra day for research for every day of writing. You also want to allow two extra days at the end of your paper to allow yourself time for revisions and polishing. This means that for a 21-page research paper, you need to allow about two and a half weeks to complete it.

21 pages divided by 3 pages a day =
7 days for writing + 7 additional days for research + 2 days revision= 16 days

Be sure to only count days you plan to actually work on the paper. If you don't want to work for sixteen consecutive days in a row, you'll have to start earlier.

For group projects, plan to meet at least three weeks before a presentation (more if it is a large scale project worth a large portion of your grade). Plan your initial group meeting as soon as you have your group assigned, even if that meeting is still weeks away, and write it in your calendar. Work on group projects goes much more slowly than individual projects because of conflicting schedules and delays in communication. You have to expect that you'll only be able to meet a few times and that you'll have to wait for group members to send around their completed part of the project. This means you have to allow a safety net of a week or so longer than you think the project should take. Therefore, your "start date" for a group project may be a month before its actual due date.

For any other type of major assignment, allow at least one day of work for every two hours of work the project will require. Remember, whether you are working alone or in a team, projects always end up taking longer than you think they will, so plan for more time than you think you'll need!

4) Look for big tests

For tests, look at how frequent they are and how much material they are likely to include. If you only have one midterm and one final, be prepared for them to be heavy-duty tests that require a lot of studying. If your tests are more frequent, know that they are likely to only include a few weeks of material. For major exams, mark in your calendar that you will start reviewing the material two weeks before the test date. For more frequent tests or quizzes, this date only needs to be a week before the day of the exam.

> ◈ Don't let an upcoming test stress you out. A large chunk of test anxiety comes from cramming material at the last minute. Start preparing early and reduce your stress!

Now, instead of experiencing Syllabus Overload, your Time Diet has given you the ability to start your semester with the confidence that everything will get done on time. All you have to do is look at your calendar that you've carefully planned in advance. You have a lot of due dates, but your calendar tells you exactly how they're all going to be met. Say goodbye to that excess end-of-semester stress.

Practice Time

Now that you understand how to properly read a syllabus, let's practice! Go get a syllabus from one of your classes. Use the sample syllabus as a model and find your *Get To Know You Assignment, Recurring Assignments, Major Projects* and *Major Tests* for that class. Write in your start dates for each one and transfer the dates to your calendar. Still need help figuring out your start dates? Refer to this easy start date calculator on the following page.

Start Date Calculator

Type of Assignment	Start Date
Get to Know You Assignment	The same day it's assigned if possible, but no later than two days after.
Recurring Assignments	No later than two days before it's due.
Major Papers	Allow one day for every three pages of writing, an additional day of research for every three pages if need be, and two days for revising.
Other Major Projects	Allow one day for every two hours of expected work.
Major Tests	Start studying two weeks before the test.
Any Other Assignments	No later than four days before the due date.

Other Deadlines to Consider

As a college student, homework assignments are not the only deadlines you need to be concerned about. Financial aid deadlines and internship and job applications are also extremely important and cannot be pushed aside. These are hard and fast deadlines that often have a big impact on your future. They are not adjustable. If you fail to meet them, your applications will not be considered. These types of deadlines include:

-**Financial aid**
-**Scholarships**
-**Jobs and internships**
-**Adding or dropping classes**
-**Credit card payments**
-**Other bills**

Just like homework, you need two dates to put in your calendar: the "due date" and the "start date." Remember, the "due date" is the absolute latest a task can be completed, but the start date is when you actually plan to do it. Make sure with important deadlines like financial aid, scholarships and internships, that the start date is as soon as possible, and no later than five days before the due date. These are important tasks you do not want to be doing at the last minute. Remember, when you wait until the last minute to get something done, you give up the control you once had over your time and risk an emergency coming up that prevents you from completing your task. If you forget to get your scholarship papers in on time, the worker at the financial aid office is not going to care that you had a cold the night before, or that you've been busy with other school work. You may have just made a thousand-dollar mistake, and there will be little you can do about it.

With serious deadlines like this, it always helps to consider the worst-case scenario. If you get a notification in your email that your new scholarship application is available and you catch yourself deciding to fill it out "later" consider what could happen. It could get buried in your inbox and you could completely forget about it. You might remember it the day before it's due, but then notice that you need three letters of recommendation. How in the world are you going to get three letters of recommendation at 11p.m.? Answer: you're not. You won't get the completed application done in time. Is that really worth it? No. Start the application well before the due date. Your ability to continue your education may depend on it.

> ❖ Scholarship deadlines are nothing to mess around with! Forgetting to get your application in on time is a horrible excuse to miss out on hundreds or thousands of dollars.

If you have your first credit card in college, make sure you get in the habit of paying off your balance every month on time. Missing credit card deadlines will not only cost you money in the short term, it may also cost you money in the long term. Continually making late payments to your card will cause you to rack up late fees and can negatively impact your credit. Your credit score may not seem important now, but when you graduate and want to buy a car it certainly will be! Carrying a balance on your card can incur steep interest charges and you certainly don't want to graduate from college with massive amounts of credit card debt. Be smart. Write these payment dates in your calendar and stick to them.

What Should My Calendar Look Like?

You now know how to use your calendar, but what should it look like? The first decision you'll have to make is whether to use a paper calendar or an electronic one. If you are new to keeping a calendar I strongly suggest using a paper one and here is why: you haven't figured out the way you like to write in your calendar yet! If you start off right away with an electronic one, you are forced to use the features the programmers give you. If you use a paper one first, you can figure out whether you like to star things, circle things, how big you like your calendar boxes to be, and where you most frequently write in it.

Once you've figured out all of these factors with your paper calendar, you're more equipped to choose an electronic calendar that suits your needs, rather than just using the one you happen to have on your smart phone.

> ◈ Remember: it doesn't matter how nice or professional a calendar looks. If you don't use it, it's worthless!

When choosing your paper calendar, you have several factors to consider. You want it to be small enough so that you can carry it with you. Your calendar needs to be with you at all times so you can write down a deadline as soon as you know about it. The longer you have to wait to note a deadline, the less likely it is going to actually make it into your calendar. You also want to make sure your calendar has a spot to clip a pen or that it's thin enough to clip a pen onto. This is essential. Remember, the goal is to make it very easy for you to write things down and if you have to search for something to write with, that adds a layer of complication.

It also helps if your calendar shows a whole month at a time so you can quickly see what your month looks like at a glance. You can't do this when you are just looking at one day or one week. I keep a pocket calendar in my purse at all times. It's about three inches wide and five inches tall. It doesn't have all the "extras" that organizers sometimes try to add to calendars like sections for notes, phone numbers, time zone charts, metric conversion charts etc… These only add extra pages to your calendar and makes it bulkier. The bigger something is, the less likely you are to carry it with you everywhere you go.

Choosing Your Digital Calendar

Once you feel comfortable using your paper calendar, there is nothing wrong with continuing to use it! (I love paper calendars because of the flexibility a pen gives me to write wherever and however I want without being constrained to boxes on a screen.) If you want to start using a digital calendar instead, I suggest you keep it on your phone, not your computer. You are far more likely to pull out your phone or tablet to enter a deadline than your whole laptop. Many programs allow you to sync your computer calendar to your phone calendar so you have the same thing in both places. That is ideal!

Make sure the calendar display is as big as possible and that it gives you maximum flexibility to type things where you want. It should only require one or two clicks to enter a new deadline. Remember: the more difficult it is to enter a deadline, the less likely you are to do it! Also, cell phone calendars often only display an icon to alert you that you have a deadline but won't display what that deadline actually is until you click on that date. Try to avoid this. Finding and displaying a deadline should be as quick and easy as possible. One of the best parts of using a digital calendar is the "alerts" function. If you are really afraid you will forget a deadline, set up an alarm to go off at a certain day and time to remind you.

The Choose-To List

Your Choose-To List is the second part of any good time management system. This is where you write down all of the tasks you plan to do on a given day. I know it seems like a pain to keep a list like this, but trust me. It's worth it! You have too much going on in your busy college life to keep track of all your obligations in your head. That being said, it is very important that you only have one Choose-To List. Oftentimes people will keep one list on their computer, one list on a piece of paper, one list on the back of their hand etc…which of course completely defeats the purpose of having a list! You have to keep everything you plan to do in one central location so that when you're done with one thing you know immediately where to look to find out what needs to be done next!

> ◆Even if you *were* able to remember everything you want to do every day, think how much easier it is to just write it down. Think of it as freeing up your brain for more important things.

Be careful not to confuse the Choose-To List with its evil twin, the "To-do" list. Calling it a "To-do" lists make it sound as though some schedule fairy is forcing us to complete certain tasks. Remember, everything you do during the day is a choice, even if it doesn't seem like it!

Making Your List

Every day you'll need to make a new list. Again, this may seem like a pain, but get over it. Organizing your time and staying on top of your school schedule is worth the 90 seconds it will take to make your list each day. Designate a time to do this every day. I like to create my Choose-To List when I'm drinking my coffee in the morning. You might like to do it before you go to sleep the night before. It doesn't matter when you do it, as long as you are consistently setting aside time to plan your day before it happens.

There are some things that may be on your list every day and others that only show up occasionally. Here are three easy steps to making your list most effective.

1. Check your Calendar

Find today's date on your calendar and see if it is the "start date" for one of your assignments. If it is, write that assignment on your Choose-To List. If you have any appointments, meetings or work shifts, add those to your list as well.

2. Look at Yesterday's Choose-to List

Is there anything you wanted to work on yesterday, but didn't get a chance to do? Add it to today's Choose-to List

3. Add any Continuing Work

What assignments have you started recently? Set yourself a small, manageable goal for this assignment and add it to your list. This could be something like "Figure out Project Topic" or " Finish 3 Stats Problems."

When you're making your Choose-To List for the day, don't forget to schedule in Desserts or fun things for yourself! You can't or won't realistically work all day long, and if you try to deprive yourself of too many fun things, you're going to feel burnt out very quickly. Then, you'll just end up putting off the work you've scheduled in order to do something relaxing. Instead, make the Desserts a part of your schedule to begin with. If you take the time to schedule fun things, then they become part of your day and won't have to take the place of work. Is your favorite T.V. show at 8:00p.m. on Thursday evenings? Great! Schedule your work around it. Picking a few Desserts to make part of your regular schedule will help you stick to your Time Diet.

Using Your List

◆Getting used to keeping your Choose-To List with you at all times may be difficult at first, especially if you aren't used to grabbing much more than your room key or ID on your way out the door. You'll get used to it!

Now that you have your list, you need to keep it with you! When you're in your apartment or dorm, your Choose-To List should live by your computer, or wherever you do your work. When you leave for class in the morning or afternoon, your Choose-To List comes with you. You need to get in the habit of taking your list with you all the time. After all, it doesn't do much good to have a list telling you what to do while you're on campus if it's in your room all day.

When you finish something on your list, cross it off and be sure to frequently refer back to the list throughout the day. Often times when we don't do something during that day that we wanted to do, it's not because we decided to procrastinate, it's because we forgot about it! Frequently checking your Choose-To List eliminates that problem.

What Do I Do First?

Sometimes when your Choose-To List is very long, figuring out where to start can be half the battle. Well, start at the beginning! Read through the list and consider your DIPs:

Deadlines, Importance, People

1) Deadlines

What things are due the soonest? Tasks with an approaching deadline need to take priority over things that aren't due for a while. Remember, ideally you won't have to worry about tasks that are due the next day because you've been doing a little bit at a time and have almost completed the task by the time the deadline approaches.

2) Importance

If you're debating between doing two things that have similar deadlines, do the most important one first. That may seem like common sense, but you'd be surprised how often students spend hours on small homework assignments while a huge project worth half their grade sits waiting to be started. If you've carefully budgeted your time, you'll have time to get it all done. Just in case though, I'd much rather have the important things done first!

3) Other People

Remember, you aren't the only one with deadlines! While you shouldn't put everyone else's needs above your own, you can't put their needs dead last either. That just isn't right or fair. Haven't you ever been in a situation where you want to move forward with something but you can't because you are waiting on something from someone else? This happens in group projects all the time. The group leader gets stuck staying up until 4:00a.m. putting a project together the night before it is due because everyone waited until the last minute to send him or her their work.

Now that you've considered your deadlines, their importance and the needs of other people, is there a DIP task that you're feeling particularly inspired to do? Remember, if you're inspired to do something, you're more likely to do a better and faster job. It is important to consider all three factors, not just one. If you only consider deadlines, you'll be in a never-ending cycle of only working on things a few days before they are due. If you only consider importance, you'll let a lot of less-important things slip through the cracks. If you only consider other people, you'll never get anything done for yourself. This is why you have to consider all three before making your decision. Maybe after considering these three things, you'll choose to work on that group project due in a few days instead of the that paper due in a few weeks that you've been dying to get started on.

Fill out the following "Choose-To List" worksheet to find out what categories your work belongs in.

Choose-To List Worksheet

Type of Task	Example
Deadlines	*An example of a task that has a deadline is:*
Importance	*An example of a task that is important is:*
People	*An example of a task that affects other people is:*
What do I feel like doing?	*I never want to do this task, so if I ever do become inspired to complete it, I should start right away!*

This whole process of deciding what things to tackle first on your Choose-To List sounds complicated, but it is really very simple. The steps outlined above only take a few seconds to do. They aren't really meant to be steps at all. Pretty soon, you'll get so good at scanning your Choose-To List and considering the three factors that it really happens all at once. Don't be intimidated! You can do it!

The 5-Minute Rule

Let's be clear about your Choose-To List. Chances are, you will most likely not accomplish everything on it and you'll more than likely add a few things to it throughout the day. This is all part of being flexible and rolling with your day. Nothing ever goes exactly according to your plan. However, before you add something to your list, ask yourself, "Can what I'm adding to my list be accomplished in five minutes or less?" If it can, don't add it to the list, just do it now!

Little five-minute tasks are Vegetables in your Time Diet. As any seven-year-old can tell you, ignoring your vegetables doesn't make them go away. The best way to get rid of them is to eat them quickly (with lots of ketchup)! When the light bulb burns out in your room or apartment, I know you don't feel like changing it, but truthfully, you aren't going to feel any more like changing it tomorrow than you do right now, so just do it. It takes all of three minutes and then it'll be done.

> ◆We spend a lot of time convincing ourselves that it's OK to put off little tasks. By the time we're done making excuses, we could have finished the task already!

The 5-Minute Rule especially applies if it has a direct impact on someone else. For example, I had a professor email me once on a Saturday asking for a three to four sentence quote from a student's perspective for a grant proposal he was writing. My first thought was, "Ugh, it's a Saturday, I'll get to this later." But then I realized, writing this quote would only take a few minutes, and he was probably spending his weekend writing this grant proposal and couldn't send it out until he had this bit of information from me. Doing this now would take very little effort on my part and would allow him to move forward with his project. Now granted, the person asking me for information was also my professor, and common sense should tell you to always do what your professors ask right away since they give you your grades. Nonetheless, the 5-Minute Rule applies no matter who is asking for something.

Remember: treat other people's time the way you want yours to be treated. The only thing more frustrating than having your work held up because you're waiting for something from another person, is knowing that the thing you're waiting for only takes five minutes to do.

What Should My List Look Like?

Now that you know how to use your Choose-To List, you'll want to make sure you have one that is easy to use! My Choose-To List is simply a small

> ◈I can't stress enough how important it is to keep a pen near your list. If you don't have a pen, you won't write things down. This is why I never lend my Choose-To List pen to anyone. Get your own!

yellow pad of paper. I like it because it is cheap and extremely portable. Remember, a Choose-To List is useless if you don't carry it around with you. You can slip your pad of paper into your school bag in the morning and go. Because it is slim, it doesn't take up a lot of space.

What About Technology?

Just like the calendar, I personally prefer to keep my Choose-To List with a paper and pen. However, if you carry your phone or computer everywhere, you may want to keep your Choose-To List in digital form. This is fine as long as it is easy to use. Make sure that it doesn't take more than a few seconds and more than one or two keystrokes to access your list. If it takes too long to get to your list, you're less likely to use it and then you're just wasting your time. Remember, only use technology if it truly makes things easier to organize. If it's faster to use paper and pencil, just do it!

Time Buckets

Now that you have your organization system set up, you'll need to figure out when to do all of the things that you have on your calendar and Choose-To List. A Choose-To List doesn't do much good if you just randomly start tackling tasks, jumping haphazardly from one to the next. This is why I like to break up my day into four to six mini days. Being faced with a long list of tasks and only 24 hours to do them can be overwhelming, but by breaking your day up into chunks, planning out these tasks becomes much more manageable.

In high school, your day was already broken up for you. You had several morning classes, then lunch, then another few classes, then maybe some sort of after school activity, and then you went home. Now, in college, your schedule may be more spread out and you'll have longer gaps of time to fill. You'll want to figure out how to use this time most

> ◈Using Time Buckets helps you see right away which parts of your day are the best times to work. Not all parts of the day are created equal!

effectively. That is why breaking up your day into chunks is so helpful. It makes scheduling your work time and your fun time much easier.

Think about your day as consisting of four to six Time Buckets. A Time Bucket is a chunk of time that you can put tasks into. Your Time Buckets will differ from day to day and will change from semester to semester as your class schedule changes.

Take a moment to think about how the chunks of your day are put together. Here is an example of what Sam the undergraduate's Time Bucket schedule may look like:

Bucket 1: 8:00a.m.-10:00a.m. Class
Bucket 2: 10:00a.m.-2:00p.m. Lunch and break
Bucket 3: 2:00p.m.-4:00p.m. Class
Bucket 4: 4:00p.m.-5:30p.m. Taekwondo club meeting
Bucket 5: 5:30p.m.-10:00p.m. Dinner/break
Bucket 6: 10:00p.m.-8:00a.m. Internet time/sleep

When Sam is deciding when to accomplish things on his Choose-To List, he can automatically eliminate Buckets 1, 3 and 4. These Buckets are already filled with obligations. Bucket 6 should also be cast aside. While a few hours of internet and relaxing time could be given up, he needs to safe-guard his sleep time. Getting enough sleep is important for staying focused and staying healthy.

So, that really leaves Buckets 2 and 5. All of the tasks on Sam's Choose-To List are going to be put in Bucket 2 from 10:00am-2:00pm or in Bucket 5 from 5:30pm-10:00pm. This will include any homework, social time, eating, errands and cleaning that needs to be done for the day.

Once Sam has his Choose-To List written for the day, how will he decide which tasks will go in which bucket?

Managing Your Time Buckets

Not all Time Buckets are created equal. Certain times of the day will be better for doing certain types of things, depending on what kind of worker you are. When deciding which tasks to accomplish when, Sam needs to consider the following:

Find which Time Bucket is the most stable and during which one you have the most energy. This is where Meat tasks and other important things go.

Sam knows that Bucket 2 from 10:00am-2:00pm is usually very stable. That is, he can generally count on having those four hours free. His friends are all in class at that time and he is unlikely to be interrupted. Because it is earlier in the day, he knows he's also likely to have more energy. So, this is where he puts his Meat tasks because he knows he'll have the energy to work through them. This is also where he puts his Vegetable tasks that fall under the DIP (Deadlines, Importance, People) category. They may not require as much thinking, but they are important and since he's unlikely to be interrupted during this Time Bucket, it's the perfect time to get them done.

Find the Time Bucket in which you usually have the least energy. This is where your particularly mindless Vegetable tasks go.

> ◈There will definitely be times you'll have to work when you're tired and don't feel like it. However, the more you can avoid it the better!

We all have those times during the day when we simply can't do anything that requires even the smallest bit of mental challenge. For Sam, that's Bucket 5. When he comes home from Taekwondo practice he's starving and exhausted. This is why after he collapses on the couch for a few minutes and eats dinner, he won't have the energy or concentration to tackle any Meat tasks. He needs to use this time to do his Vegetable tasks. This would be a perfect time to make his flashcards or outlines to help him study for his midterm next week, or to scrub all the dishes in the sink while listening to his favorite music. After a few Vegetable tasks, this is also the Time Bucket into which Sam will put his Desserts. Sam loves to surf the Internet and play computer games so as soon as he's done with his Vegetable tasks he'll retreat to his computer until it's time to go to bed.

If you're thinking that creating and analyzing your Time Buckets is over-kill, you're wrong. Productive and efficient students know that if they want to get the most amount of work done in the least amount of time, timing is everything. Trying to do difficult work when you're tired takes longer and wastes your time. You do your best work when you are fresh.

Determining Your Own Time Buckets

Now it's time to figure out how you're going to break up your own Time Buckets. Remember, they will change from semester to semester and probably even from day to day. I want you to think of tomorrow's schedule and base your Time Buckets on that. Look for natural blocks in your schedule based around things such as meals, classes, club meetings and other obligations. Then use the chart on the following page to break up your day.

Time Bucket Chart

Number	Time Span	Energy Level 1= no energy 10= tons of energy	What happens in this Time Bucket?
1.	___:___ to ___:___		
2.	___:___ to ___:___		
3.	___:___ to ___:___		
4.	___:___ to ___:___		
5.	___:___ to ___:___		
6.	___:___ to ___:___		

Now that you've figured out your Time Buckets for one day, use this same process to break up your other days. Pretty soon this process will become second nature. You'll be breaking up your day into chunks and analyzing them according to your energy level while hardly thinking about it.

Review

Good job! Now you know how to organize your schedule so you can quickly and easily keep track of what needs to be done and when you're going to do it. Let's review what we've talked about:

1) You don't need to be super-organized to manage your time. You just need two things: a Choose-To List for daily tasks and a pocket calendar for long-term deadlines.

2) Start dates are just as important as due dates. Don't let your obsession with deadlines cause Syllabus Overload. Calmly plan out when you will begin each project.

3) When deciding what to accomplish, consider your DIPs: Deadlines (when a task is due), Importance (how important a task is) and People (does this task affect others?)

4) If something takes five minutes or less, do it now rather than adding it to your Choose-To List for later.

5) Break up your day into Time Buckets. Staring down a 24 hour day can be overwhelming, especially if you have a long Choose-To List. Break it up into a few "mini-days" to make it more manageable.

A successful Time Diet takes self-control and discipline, but all the self-control in the world won't help you if you can't keep track of what you're doing! A simple, consistent system of organization is vital to good time management. Now that you have your system, you're ready to start putting it to good use!

Emily Schwartz

PART 3
GETTING IT ALL DONE

Emily Schwartz

Your Time Diet is progressing wonderfully! You have now adjusted your attitude about time management and have your organization system in place. Congratulations! Now you're moving on to the third and final step in your diet: actually getting your work done. In a regular diet, there are two basic steps to lose weight, eat less and exercise more. Similarly, in your Time Diet there are two ways to get rid of extra fat in your schedule:

1. Do less
2. Do it more efficiently

You've already eliminated any tasks that aren't necessary in Part 1, so you've already taken care of "Do Less." Now you need to focus on doing the rest of your work more efficiently so it fits into a smaller amount of time. This might sound intimidating because you may already feel overwhelmed and wish for more hours in the day as it is. This leads us to Myth #4:

Myth #4: I Don't Have Time To Get it All Done

Remember, half the stress of getting it all done comes from worrying about getting it all done. "Worrying" and "stressing out" are not tasks you have the time or energy for. My mom had a story she liked to tell me when she saw me stressing about schoolwork.

"Two cows were faced with an immense pasture of grass to graze. The first cow stood in awe before it and said, 'How in the world will I ever finish all this grass? There is surely far too much here for me.' The second cow said nothing, put her head down, and started grazing."

In college, your goal is to be the second cow. You want to focus on actually getting things done rather than stressing about the work that still lies in front of you. Besides, you've already planned out when you're going to start all that work, and how you are going to make time to complete it, so what do you have to worry about?

Josh

Josh was one of my very good friends in my master's program. Josh's problem was that he was definitely the first cow in my story, not the second cow. He was what I like to call a "Stresser" because I'm pretty sure stressing out was one of his favorite activities. He enjoyed hearing about the stressful parts of other people's days. It was almost as though he fed on stress: his own and others'! The funny thing was, Josh had a pretty easy schedule compared to most of our classmates. He was working less than part-time, and only taking two classes. Most people working part-time take three or four!

Still, Josh simply could not take his relatively easy schedule for what it was. He stressed out about everything. Every reading assignment was too long and he didn't know how he was going to finish it. Every project was too complicated. Every test or quiz was a nightmare to be feared. I wanted so badly to shake him and say, "Calm down! Just start doing the work instead of complaining about it!"

> ◆Friends are great support systems in college, but constantly complaining to them about your workload is toxic. Complaining about stress only breeds more stress!

Much like the "Busy Body" attitude from Part 1, I understand the appeal of Josh's "Stresser" attitude. In college, being stressed out is almost a badge of honor. Don't get caught up in that game. You're smarter than that now. Don't get drawn into a "Busy Battle," where people go back and forth trying to "one-up" each other with how busy they are. You now know that being busy means nothing. Being productive means everything.

Mentally Fighting Stress

Stress is a natural part of life and all college students will feel it at some point during the semester. We want to do our best and we worry we won't be able to measure up. So, what do you do when you feel that wave of stress coming on? I find it's best to first tackle stress mentally. For many years of my life, I played the piano and the oboe and frequently performed in public recitals. I had to quickly learn to control my stress level before a big public performance. I realized that 90% of the stress and anxiety I felt in the days leading up to a performance was self-inflicted. I allowed my mind to worry about making a mistake, which in turn stressed me out. People would always tell me, "Just don't think about it!" Of course, one of the easiest ways to ensure that something will constantly remain on your mind is to try not to think about it! Instead I tried to actually convince myself that I wasn't worried about it. This was not always easy. Whenever I started psyching myself out for failure I had to say, "Why would I be stressed about this? I am the most calm and collected person in the world." It sounds crazy, but with enough conviction, it works.

The same is true for stressing about a workload. We all know when our busiest, most stress-inducing times are. It's those few weeks leading up to the end of a semester when it can feel like everything is crashing down on us at once! Tests! Projects! Finals! It can cause your inner "Stresser" to run wild! Remember to just calm down, focus, and put your head down and start grazing.

Physically Tackling Stress

Once you have mentally tackled your stress, there are several things you can physically do to help keep stress at bay.

1) Exercise. Make time in your schedule for physical activity.
2) Get enough sleep. Running on too little sleep can severely impact your stress level.
3) Drink plenty of water. Carry a water bottle with you to make sure you stay hydrated.
4) Meditate. Turn off your cell phone, close your Internet browser and give yourself a few quiet moments to relax.
5) Eat right. Making a habit of skipping lunch and devouring fast food for dinner may be convenient, but it doesn't help your stress.
6) Listen to music. Your favorite tunes have a way of instantly relaxing you.
7) Take a walk. Even a quick lap around the quad can help calm you down.
8) Call a friend. Sometimes just chatting with a friend can get your mind off of your stress. That's what friends are for!

Time Killers

So, you've put your stress aside and have sat down to begin tackling some work. Good for you! Now, you have to maintain that focused attitude by watching out for Time Killers. Time Killers are those little things that distract us from our work without our permission. Some common Time Killers are social networking sites, email, snacking, texting, T.V. and so on. These things aren't necessarily bad by themselves, but when they disrupt us from our work, they can be toxic. For example, texting is a quick and fun way to communicate, but how many times have you been trying to work on homework and then BAM! All of a

> ◆The difference between a Time Killer and a break is that breaks are planned, Time Killer aren't. Don't let these little additions break your focus without your permission.

sudden you're texting your friend. It's as though your cell phone just jumped into your hand without your permission. Now, instead of working, you're reading about how bored your friend is in class.

The trick to dealing with Time Killers is recognizing that they are things you enjoy doing and scheduling a separate time to do them. For example, if your major Time Killer is snacking, plan for that before you start your work. Bring a small snack to your desk that will take a long time to eat. When that snack is done, you're done. No more impromptu trips to the vending machines to distract you from your focus.

How can you cope with your own Time Killers? Use the following chart to help you figure out a plan of attack for common Time Killers and add your own at the bottom.

Time Killer Worksheet

Time Killer	How I can prevent this Time Killer from interfering with my work.
1. Texting	*Turn phone to silent or leave it far away from you while working*
2. Social networking/email	*Turn off your internet connection while you're working to resist the temptation*
3. T.V	*Do your work in a room that doesn't have a T.V, or turn your desk so you can't see it. If you can't see it, you'll be less likely to want to watch it.*
4.	
5.	
6.	

Don't Let Work Take Longer Than it Should

Focused, uninterrupted work is the key to getting more done in a shorter amount of time. After all, tasks have a way of expanding to fill whatever time you've set aside to finish them. This phenomenon is known as Parkinson's Law. Pretend that the box below represents the three hours you have given yourself to complete an assignment. Chances are your work will expand to take up the whole box no matter how little time it actually requires.

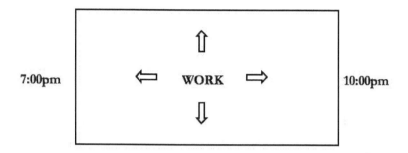

This is because you will be very tempted to fill all that extra time with Time Killers.

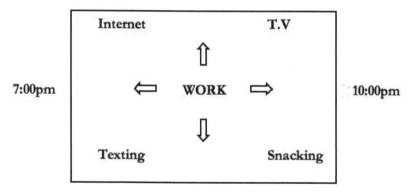

However, now that you're being smart about your Time Killers, you won't have all those little interruptions and your work won't take as long. You'll be amazed at how much faster you'll be able to get work done without all those little interruptions. You'll also start to get a more realistic idea of how long your homework actually takes. A homework assignment that used to take you three hours may now only take you one. Now your evening can look like this instead:

Instead of letting little Time Killers expand your work time, you can spend one focused hour on homework, and then you'll have two hours to do whatever Dessert task you like! You could even choose to use those two hours to text your friends, check your email or do other Time Killer tasks that you can now actually enjoy without feeling guilty that they are distracting you from your work!

Maximize Your Reading Time

When I ask college students what type of homework takes up the biggest chunk of their time, the answer is almost always "reading." Reading is a huge part of many college classes, especially classes where your grade is primarily based on a midterm and a final. The trick is to absorb the most from your reading in the quickest amount of time. This will not only make your reading go faster, but it will also cut down on your studying time at the end of the semester because you won't have to review as much. Follow these tips to cut down on the time you have to devote to reading assignments.

1) Make sure you are focused

Have you ever sat down to read something for class and then suddenly realized that you're five pages ahead of where you started but your mind wandered and you have no idea what you've just read? This happens to all of us and it's the direct result of a lack of focus. Reading without focus is a waste of your time because you'll just have to end up reading it again!

It is important to remember that reading requires both visual *and* auditory skills. This means that the comprehension of what we read comes from hearing the words in our head in addition to seeing the words on the page. Therefore, if we have other thoughts swimming around in our head it is impossible to "hear" the words we read. This is why it's impossible to concentrate on reading while you're also trying to eavesdrop on a conversation in the next room (not that I've done that...)

Help yourself stay focused by removing distractions. Some people can easily concentrate with music or some sort of background noise, while others need silence. Find out which kind of person you are by trying both. Never read for school while in a reclined position, such as on your couch or bed. The temptation to nod off and fall asleep is too great! Save comfy couch reading for fun books and magazines. For school reading, find a desk to work at where nothing else is in your direct peripheral vision, even if this means simply putting the rest of your work on the floor or closing your laptop.

When other work catches your eye while you're trying to read, it is easy to let that work take over your thoughts and distract your from your reading.

2) Always read with a pen, not a highlighter

> ◆Reading a book that isn't yours? Don't use pen on library books! Use sticky notes instead so you can still mark main ideas and jot things down.

Reading with a pen keeps you engaged with the text, and if you're engaged you're far more likely to stay focused. If you have a reaction to something you read, instantly write it down. I often write, "No!" in the margins if I disagree with something, or "Really???" if I find something hard to believe. Marking up your reading also helps you save time with studying and reviewing later. When you come to a main point or major idea, use your pen to circle it and then quickly jot down why you think it's important. This way, when you're reviewing for a test or class discussion you can save time by quickly accessing the important points, rather than having to re-read the entire document. I recommend using a pen rather than a highlighter. Highlighters are good at quickly bringing my attention back to something, but I often forget why I highlighted it. With a pen, I can quickly underline something important, put a star in the margin to easily see where it is, and then jot a word or two down to remind myself why I felt this was important. Pens convey more information than highlighters do.

3) Recognize that not every word is important

Think of the reading in front of you as a giant field of gravel pebbles interspersed with nuggets of gold. If you were to pick up each individual rock you saw and carefully examine it to determine whether it was gravel or gold, you would be in the field forever. The key to finding the gold the fastest is to quickly pass over the gravel and head right for the shiny stuff. So it is with reading too. Not every word you read is important to your overall understanding of the topic. You need to seek out the "nuggets" of importance and skim over the "gravel" that rounds out each paragraph. It is usually easiest to find the important concepts in business writing, which tends to be very clear and to-the-point (though not always!) Pay close attention to section headings, graphs and anything brought up in the introduction (as this usually indicates that the author thinks it is important). Look for sentences that specifically persuade, explain or compare concepts. Skim over background information, which is usually not as important to your overall understanding.

It can be a little more difficult to find the main concepts in "academic writing" such as in the humanities and social sciences. It includes more details and flowery writing. In this case, it is best to focus on the first and last sentence of a paragraph, which usually gives you a pretty good indication of whether the paragraph is important or not. Remember, when reading material for a test it is important to ask yourself, "What does my professor want me to gain from this?" rather than, "What do I want to gain from this?" After all, while your own critical thinking skills are important, your professor is the one writing the test! Look for sentences that specifically define certain concepts, explain how they are different from each other, and why they are important. Look for sections labeled "results," "conclusions" or "summary" and read them intently. This is where the most important information is.

4) Quiz yourself

I find it's very helpful when professors give periodic announced quizzes throughout the semester to make sure the class is staying on top of the reading. You'll find this far more prevalent in undergraduate than graduate school. If your professor doesn't do that, make your own quiz to make sure you understand the material! Your self-made quiz doesn't have to be anything elaborate. Just ask yourself, "If I were giving my class a quiz on this reading, what would I ask them?" Take a quick moment to jot down

> ◆ It is important to periodically make sure you are understanding what you're reading. However, if something really doesn't make sense after a few readings, ask your professor before you spend too much time trying to wrestle with it on your own.

answers to broad questions such as, "What is the overall importance of this reading to our class topic?" "What are the main themes or concepts discussed here?" and "Who are the main people associated with these concepts?"

Cutting the Fat from Your Studying

Now that you know how to get the most out of your class reading the first time, you'll only need to review the information, not re-learn it, before test day. This will dramatically cut down on your study time. The trick to reviewing for a test efficiently is to know exactly what is going to be tested so you don't waste your time reviewing unnecessary information. This unessential information is "fat" in your studying that eats up time and keeps you in the library until 2:00a.m. There is no room in your Time Diet for unnecessary work!

The best way to find out exactly what is on a test is to ask your professor! So many students fail to do this because they are afraid of looking stupid. Asking what you should focus on while studying is a reasonable question. If your professor replies with a vague answer such as, "Chapters 2-11, just like it says in the syllabus," don't give up hope! Professors test what they think is important and it's fairly easy to judge what they think is important based on what they focus on or give particular attention to in class.

In all testing situations, regardless of your professor, there are a few general rules regarding what to expect on an important test that can guide your review process and save you time.

Writing Finals

Any test that involves history, liberal arts or even science is likely to have a long essay and short answer section. To make the most efficient use of your studying time, focus on the following four things:

1) Evolution of key concepts through time

In any class that has even a small history component, there is almost always an essay question that says, "Trace the evolution of (blank) from (insert year) to (insert year) citing specific examples from your readings and lectures." Learn to expect this and immediately recognize when information might lend itself to this kind of question.

2) Comparison of key terms

Don't simply make a list of key terms, define them and read them over and over until you've committed them to memory. This is what middle school teachers expect of their students. In college, professors expect your knowledge to go deeper. It's more important to focus on how key terms relate to each other. Instead of simply creating a definition list, link different terms together and explain how they are either the same or different.

3) Why events/concepts are important

Another deficiency of the memorized definition list is that it ignores why key concepts are important. For example, it is not enough to know when or how the Spanish/American War started. More importantly, you need to be able to state its impact on world history.

4) Specific contributions of key people

It is important to know who the important people are in your reading and what they contributed to your field of study. On your American Lit final it is less important to know where F. Scott Fitzgerald was born and how many books he wrote. It is more important to know how his books contributed to American Literature.

"Doing" Finals

Tests that require you to do something other than writing, such as solving a problem, require a different method of studying. Classes in fields such as math or engineering typically have "doing" finals.

1) Keep up with homework

If your professor doesn't collect homework, there can be a strong temptation to not do it. Always do your homework! Taking an hour each week to complete your homework is far better than trying to learn a whole semester's worth of material right before a final exam. The time to realize you don't understand a concept is the day after it's brought up in class, not the day before the final. Remember, studying is a Meat task and needs to be spread out rather than tackled all at once in a few days.

2) Practice

The best way to study for a "doing" final is to practice doing what you'll be asked to do! As obvious as this may sound, students often fail to do this. Instead they focus on definitions, formulas, and reviewing their homework. This is not the best use of your time! The questions on math tests that are worth the most points aren't the ones that ask you to recite formulas, they are the ones that ask you to apply the formulas. Also, a professor is not likely to ask you a question that you already completed for homework. Instead of using your time to memorize or review what you've already done, use your time to practice new problems. Look back through your homework for what kinds of problems your professor has asked you to do. Then, find problems similar to them in your book that you haven't done yet and work through them. Remember, you are likely to take longer to do problems on test day because you'll be a little nervous. This is why practicing is so important.

3) Explain a problem to a non-major

A sure sign that you've mastered a concept is if you are able to break it down into simple parts and explain it to someone who is not studying the same subject as you. Ask your art history major roommates if you can explain an engineering concept to them. If you are unable to explain what you are doing and why you're doing it to a novice, then you probably don't have a good enough command of your subject yet.

Use Study Groups Carefully

I urge you to beware of the "study group"! Collaborating with a few people to help review material can sometimes be a great way to clear up confusion and work through problems, but more often than not it ends up being a waste of time. Usually, studying with more people takes more time because everyone wants a chance to speak and give their input and there are more opportunities for distraction. I know sitting around the coffee shop with your friends makes studying sound more appealing, but plan on it taking twice as long as it would if you did it by yourself. The other problem with group studying is that there is always one person who is more prepared than everyone else. This person ends up pulling everyone else along and doesn't really learn anything.

> ◆I have never been to a study group that was a valuable use of my time. If you catch yourself at a study group that isn't helping you at all, just leave.

If you simply must study with a group, insist that everyone in your group first do the bulk of their studying on their own. Then use the group time to quiz each other and clear up any lingering questions. Make sure you have a thought-out "agenda" for your review session so you stay on track. Also, set a time limit—perhaps one or two hours—so your group time doesn't go on forever. Keep in mind that not all of your friends are also good study partners. If your study group isn't working, don't study with those people again. Just politely say that you think you get more done on your own.

Tackling Homework - Spread Out the Difficulty

As we talked about in Part One, it's sometimes difficult to motivate ourselves to do our homework. When all the homework we have to do are Meat tasks, it becomes even more difficult and we're tempted to procrastinate. In order to have a balanced diet of homework you need to spread out the difficulty. It's tempting to do the easy parts of all our homework one day leaving all of the difficult parts for another day. We've all been in that situation before. We begin one assignment with every intention to finish it, but then it gets difficult. We glance over at our Choose-To List and start another assignment instead. Then this one also gets difficult and we move on to something else. This method of frequently going back and forth between assignments is dangerous because soon you are left with a lot of half-completed work. Not only that, but the easy parts of these assignments are finished, leaving you with only the difficult parts of all of them. Now it's even harder to motivate yourself to sit down and do your homework because you know that only difficult things await!

Think of completing homework like running a race. It doesn't do any good to stretch, warm up, run the first few miles and then press the "pause button" right before your first big hill. You need all of that momentum from the warm-up and first few miles to get over that hill. The same is true for completing a difficult homework assignment. If you do all of the easy things first and stop right before the difficult part, it is much more difficult to motivate yourself to come back to it later, let alone to get back in the "concentration zone" again!

If you do need to stop a homework assignment midway through, I find it is helpful to stop while you still have one more easy task to do. For example, when you're writing a big paper and you feel yourself coming to a mental block, stop one paragraph before you're out of things to say. This way, when you come back to it later, you know that you'll have at least one easy, pre-formed paragraph in your head to write that will help give you momentum to push past the mental block. You will be much more likely to work on it later if you

◆ There is a difference between frustration and difficulty. If something beyond your control is not working or becoming frustrating, it's often best to walk away and work on something else before you let your frustration ruin your whole day.

know that you're able to sit down and immediately write a few easy sentences rather than starting off trying to write something that is proving difficult.

Start in the Middle

It's harder to motivate yourself to do homework if you know it's going to be difficult. What makes this doubly cruel is that in the case of papers or other writing assignments, the first page is often the hardest to write! How in the world are you going to motivate yourself to start a paper when you know that cursor is blinking away on that first big empty blank page and you don't have any idea where to start?

◆ If you get an idea for your project, even if you're working on something completely different, write it down. You'll never remember it when you need it later.

Try starting in the middle, not at the beginning! The first few introductory paragraphs are sometimes easier to write once you've already got some of your ideas down. After you've sketched a brief outline of your paper, start writing one of the middle paragraphs that you can more clearly visualize. This will make starting your paper much easier and you won't have that intimidating blank page staring back at you anymore. Remember, time management is equally about motivation management and you're much more motivated to continue something once you've started it.

Avoid Homework Catastrophes

One of the hardest lessons a college student (or quite frankly, anyone who uses a computer) has to learn is the consequences of forgetting to hit "save" while writing important papers. If your computer crashes and you haven't been saving regularly, you'll end up re-writing huge sections of your paper (if not the whole thing) and that is an atrocious, frustrating waste of time. You've just become an expert on breaking up your homework into manageable chunks and motivating yourself to do it. Now you don't want to waste all your precious time re-doing it because of an avoidable mistake.

Hit "Save" all the time. You should be clicking it every few minutes to make sure you don't lose anything. Also, you should be regularly backing up your hard drive. That seems like a pain...until your computer crashes and you lose everything. This happened to me my during junior year the week before finals. I was working on something on my laptop and it just froze and shut down. The hard drive was completely fried and the computer store was unable to salvage anything. Luckily, I had just started backing up my files a few weeks prior and didn't end up losing anything terribly important. I was able to load all of my school files, pictures and music right on to my new computer. If I hadn't backed them up, it would have been nearly impossible to recreate everything I'd lost. Make backing up your files a habit. It only takes a few minutes and it could save you tons of time, aggravation and headache later.

Empty Time

If you still think you have too much to do and not enough time, consider how to utilize any unexpected "empty time" during your day. I'm not talking about that three-hour block of time you have between classes on Thursday. I mean those little ten or fifteen minute segments of free time that crop up unexpectedly. This could be when you find yourself ready for class a few minutes early, when you're waiting in line at the ATM or campus bookstore or when a class is surprisingly canceled. You never know when empty time will come up so you have to be prepared to not let those precious moments go to waste!

> ◆ If you added up all the wasted minutes in your day, you'd have quite a chunk of time! If you don't want to use that time to work, at least use it to purposefully relax instead of just puttering around.

Don't know what to do with those few extra minutes? Use the handy list on the next page to get you started:

Ten Things You Can Do in Ten Minutes or Less of Empty Time

1) Make a copy of your chapter outlines or other study material and stash them in your bag. Whip them out if you are waiting in a long line or if your bus is late.

2) Get a jump-start on your Choose-To List for tomorrow.

3) Clean out your backpack or school bag. Throw away random trash or old papers that may be lurking in there.

4) Call home. You know your mom or dad likes to call and "check in" at the least convenient times. Beat them to it and earn a few brownie points. They don't have to know you had nothing better to do!

5) Pick up the clothes on your dorm room or apartment floor. It only takes a minute and you'll be more likely to do laundry later if all your dirty clothes are in one place.

6) Outline part of a paper. Carry a small notebook around with you so if you have a few minutes you can sketch out some ideas for whatever paper you need to write next.

7) Clean the dishes in the sink. If you find yourself ready for class a few minutes early wash and put away your breakfast dishes so you won't have to do it later.

8) Run a quick errand. If your class gets out a few minutes early, why not swing by the campus bookstore and pick up those exam booklets you need so you don't have to make a separate trip later.

9) Take a brisk walk. Even if it's only for ten minutes, it will help energize you for the rest of your day.

10) Read a book or glance at the news. Don't become one of those college students who reads for class all the time but never reads for fun or has no idea what is happening in the world. Don't say you don't have time. Yes, you do.

De-Clutter Your Desk

Remember, the key to getting more done in a shorter amount of time is to focus. It's much easier to focus when you are working at a clean workspace. If you're trying to work with piles of books and papers around you, you're more likely to start thinking of work you have to do for another class, or other obligations you might have. Not only that, but if you have to move piles of things off your desk to have room to work, you're far less likely to actually start your work than if that space was already available.

If you're anything like me, your desk is in a constant state of chaos. This is why when my friend and I got our own apartment our second year of college, we liked to spread out and do a lot of our work at the kitchen table. Not only was it bigger than our desks, but it was much easier to keep clear than our desks were.

If you are in a dorm room, or don't have a laptop computer that's portable, that's OK! Instead, reserve a portion of your room or desk for clutter. If you're a messy person, you'll have much more success keeping a clear space to work if you also give yourself a place to put your mess. Dorm rooms are small, I know. Even if you put a piece of masking tape down the middle of your desk and vow to keep clutter on one side and work on the other, it'll be a step in the right direction.

Take Care of Yourself

Another way to stay focused is to take care of yourself and get enough sleep. The concept of the "Freshman 15" is famous because it's true. New college students tend to eat terribly and sleep very little. There is no place for these behaviors in your Time Diet! Sure, you will sometimes stay out late with your friends, but if stay up until 3:00a.m. one night, get to bed early the next night.

> ◆ When I'd call it an early night in college, my friends used to tell me, "There's plenty of time to sleep when you're dead!" My response to that morbid comment was always, "Yes, but I'd like to have the energy to finish my degree in this lifetime thank you very much."

If you stay up late night after night you will eventually crash and your whole work schedule will suffer. It just isn't worth it!

Take advantage of the campus gym if you have one. I guarantee that you're likely to never live as close or have easy access to a gym like this again once you leave college, so use it now! Even a 20-minute burst of exercise can help focus your brain and give you a boost of energy. The gym's not your thing? Find a friend to take a jog with you around campus or get a group of friends together for a game of football or Ultimate Frisbee on the lawn. Staying active doesn't need to take a lot of time and it does wonders for your focus and energy level!

Cleaning…the Brussels Sprouts of Tasks

This part of the book has talked a lot about finding ways to get your homework done quickly, but let's not forget there are other things to worry about in college that don't involve homework! One of the biggest tasks that college students neglect or put off until the infamous "later" is cleaning. This is because there is no "Cleaning Professor" who tells you to clean your dishes by Monday or "Laundry TA" who tells you half of your grade will be based on getting up off the couch and washing your jeans. The only person who is even going to ask you about these things is probably your mother and unless she lives with you, it's easy to say, "Yeah Mom, I'm doing my laundry every week" as you pull on your dirty socks for the third day in a row.

I know that there are about a thousand things that you'd rather be doing with your time than cleaning, so that's why you have to figure out how to do it quickly and efficiently. Cleaning is a Vegetable task. Not only is it a Vegetable task, it's a Brussels sprouts task: the least appealing of all Vegetables. Remember the wise advice that every 7-year old knows? The best way to stomach Brussels sprouts (after your parents force you to) is to drown them in ketchup and swallow them

> ❖Having a clean bathroom will not exactly help improve your college GPA, but it will help you become a responsible adult. I wish I had formed better cleaning habits in college so my adjustment to my first "post college" home wasn't so difficult.

quickly in one gulp. The more time you take chewing the more time you actually have to taste them. You have to do the same with cleaning. I'm not suggesting you drown your apartment in ketchup. What I am suggesting is that you find a way to make it fun and make it fast.

Compared to your homework, cleaning is easy to do and relatively mindless. You can do it while listening to music, watching TV, or chatting on the phone with your friend. The problem is, if you don't stay on top of it and put it off for weeks and weeks, it becomes a Meat task. Meat tasks are more difficult and take longer to complete. Once you've let cleaning become a Meat task, you are even less likely to get it done.

The good news is, it only takes a few minutes a day to keep your living place clean. Whether you live in an apartment, a dorm room or a rented house with your friends, keeping your place clean is easy. Getting into the habit of cleaning now will help you make the transition from college to life-on-your-own when that time comes!

Laundry

The best thing you can do to keep your living space clean is to stay ahead of your laundry. Dirty clothes can quickly pile up on your floor and make your room both cluttered and stinky. Here are a few quick ways to make doing laundry easier.

1) Buy durable clothing
Before you buy a new piece of clothing, check the label. If it says "Hand Wash" or "Dry Clean Only," stay away! These items will be a pain to keep clean and will therefore stay on your bedroom floor longer.

2) Keep a supply of quarters
If you have to search for the quarters to do your laundry, you won't want to do it. My roommate was a genius. At the beginning of the year she took 50 dollars to the bank and changed it into quarters. That may seem like a lot of money, but you're spending it anyway. Now she never had to search for quarters for the rest of the semester!

3) Hang clothes up right away
As soon as you take your clothes out of the dryer, hang them up. This will keep them from getting wrinkled and save you the need for ironing later.

4) Put dirty clothes into a laundry bag
As clothes get dirty, put them right into a laundry bag. This way, when it's laundry time, you won't have to search all over your room collecting dirty clothes, or pick through a hamper. You can just grab the bag and go.

5) Have a schedule
To keep laundry from piling up, wash your sheets and towels one week and then your clothing the next. If you wait until the end of the month to try to wash everything at once, you'll end up with a marathon laundry session.

Cleaning Your Dorm

There are a lot of advantages to dorm living. After all, you don't have a bathroom or a kitchen to worry about! However, because dorm rooms are so small, they can be difficult to keep cleaned and organized. If you're not careful, they can quickly become giant closets that you just throw all your junk into. This is why it's important to make time to keep it organized before it becomes too overwhelming. Here are a few tips to keep your space organized in as little time as possible.

1) Have fewer things

Dorms are small places. The more things you have the more you have to straighten up and organize. Do you really need that toaster oven on your shelf? Chances are you aren't supposed to have it anyway!

2) Use plastic crates

Plastic crates were practically designed for college students. They are cheap, they stack and you can throw almost anything into them. Remember, if your system of organization takes a lot of time, you won't want to do it, so keep it simple!

3) Discuss cleaning with your roommate

Establishing your expectations of cleanliness with your roommate early will help prevent fights later on.

4) Never, *ever* put a soda in the freezer

This may or may not be a common problem, but I list it in honor of my college roommate. If you, like we did, have a habit of putting your soda can in the freezer for a few minutes to quickly get it cold, don't do it! You WILL forget to take it out and it WILL explode and cause a huge sticky frozen mess and it WILL take a good chunk of your afternoon to clean up.

Weekly Routines to Keep Your Dorm Clean

While it may not seem like you have a lot of things to keep track of, remember that in the dorm you are in close quarters with another person. Your mess becomes something your roommate has to look at every day. Don't be that kind of person! Keeping your side of the room picked up does not have to take a long time, especially now that you have great time management skills. Each of the following things takes ten minutes and you can do them on whichever day of the week you choose.

1) Pick up all your clothes on the floor

Put dirty ones in a hamper and hang up clean ones. This may sound obvious but many students don't do it!

2) Clear off the papers from your desk

Even if you don't have a perfect filing system to keep them organized, put them in a bin or file folder so they aren't making a mess.

3) Wipe down the fridge

If you have a small refrigerator, it can get really gross pretty quickly. Remember to frequently wipe the shelves down with a paper towel and throw out food that is no longer good.

4) Take out the trash

I've seen some dorm rooms that have heaping piles of trash everywhere because no one wants to walk down the hall and dump it out. Never let it get to that stage. When your trash is full, empty it.

5) Dust

Dorm rooms are dust magnets for some reason. Use a cloth or dust-buster to go over surfaces frequently so dust does not pile up. Before you buy your own bulky vacuum, see if your residence all has one you can borrow when you need it.

Adding these five things to your Choose-To List every week will keep your dorm room orderly and never let a huge mess pile up! Staying on top of easy Vegetable cleaning tasks ensures they don't become difficult Meat tasks that eat up more of your valuable time.

Apartment/House Living

Ah, the college apartment. Whether you've just "upgraded" from a dorm, or whether you managed to skip the fabulous experience of living in a 10x10 room with a total stranger, your first college apartment is very exciting. While you'll find that an apartment provides far more living space, it comes with more things to keep clean. In fact, you may realize you have taken for granted all the things your parents did to keep your childhood home clean. Having your own apartment can be a little bit of a wake-up call as to what "adult life" is really like. Not to worry. You have more than enough time in your Time Diet to handle it!

> ◆Getting your first college apartment is a momentous occasion, but it comes with a lot of added responsibilities. Nothing will make you miss your communal dorm bathroom more than the first time you have to unclog the shower or toilet!

Keeping an apartment in order is not difficult and does not have to take a lot of time. You can do this by having your cleaning supplies handy, creating a cleaning routine and staying on top of it. Here is your cleaning checklist for your apartment:

Apartment Cleaning Supplies

1) All-purpose cleaner. Keep this in the kitchen under your sink.

2) Dish brush with a handle. You'll be much more likely to use this than a sponge to clean your dishes because it keeps you away from the dirt (silly, I know, but it works!)

3) Dish Soap. Having a dishwasher in an apartment is a luxury you may not have. You may be washing your dishes by hand. Even if you have a dishwasher, you'll be washing pots and pans in the sink.

4) Glass cleaner. Keep this under your bathroom sink.

5) Sponge, paper towels and tile cleaner. Keep these with the glass cleaner under your bathroom sink.

6) Assorted rags. Rags are great for everything! They can dry dishes, dust your TV and clean up spills. Just makes sure you wash them frequently (and only use clean rags to dry your dishes!)

College students tend to not clean because they think it takes too much time; time they'd rather use doing something fun. The Time Diet is all about doing things more efficiently and choosing productive tasks during the day. Cleaning is a Vegetable task that you don't have to think too much about. Take advantage of this! Here are some easy steps to maintain your college apartment every day while also doing something enjoyable.

The Daily T.V. Cleaning Ritual

The typical half-hour T.V. show is really only 22.5 minutes long. The rest is commercials. Find a half-hour show that you like to watch. During the commercials, do the following:

1st Commercial: Wash the dishes. If you and your roommate have been diligent, you shouldn't really have too many dirty dishes after only one day. For example, you might only have three plates, three utensils, maybe a few glasses, maybe a bowl, and maybe a few pots and pans. Wash them with your dish soap, warm water and your brush with a handle. Set them on a clean dish towel or rag to dry.

2nd Commercial: Spray the all-purpose cleaner on the counters and stove. Wipe it all down with a rag.

3rd Commercial: Dry the dishes and put them away. (Make sure you are using a different rag than the one you wiped down the counters with!)

Now, your show should be over and your kitchen should be clean! Commercials are a great way to force yourself to do work. After a few times of doing this, you may realize that you're only doing around eight minutes of work and choose to just get that out of the way first and then sit down to enjoy your whole TV show. It's up to you.

Once a Week Cleaning Things

Not everything in the apartment needs to be cleaned every day. There are some things that only need to be done once a week. At first it may seem like you should just save every task you need to do for one particular day of the week, but I wouldn't recommend it. What happens if you have a study group that day? Or a big project to do? Or a fun social thing? It's better to spread out your cleaning over the whole week so if you have to miss a day it's easier to make it up on another day. Here is a suggested weekly cleaning schedule to keep you on track. Each of these lists takes only fifteen minutes or less. Don't wince: I know you have fifteen minutes to spare in your day!

Monday: Wipe down the bathroom. Without regular cleaning, your bathroom will get really gross fast. Using the paper towels and glass cleaner, wipe down the mirror. Spray the tile cleaner on your counter and shower. Let it sit for a minute and then wipe them down with the sponge.

Tuesday: Dust off the TV and other surfaces in your place such as picture frames, book cases, computer monitors and desks. Dust can pile up quickly and aggravate your allergies.

Wednesday: Do your laundry. One week, do your towels and sheets. The next week, do your clothes. The more your laundry piles up, the less likely you are to want to do it. Stay on top of your laundry and you will only be doing one load a week, not three or four.

Thursday: Take out the trash. Ideally, you would just take this out when you need to, but it's a good idea to set aside a day for it so you don't forget. Before you take out the trash, look around the apartment for anything else that should be thrown out. Also, don't forget about the trashcans in your bathroom or by your desk!

Friday: Pick up random clutter around the apartment and put it away. Even if you only have time to pick up ten things off the floor, it will help keep your place from becoming a piled up mountain of old papers and empty soda cans.

Forming Good Habits

Even though having a clean place may not be important to you now, it probably will be when you graduate from college and you have your first "real" place. It's better to form good cleaning habits now so that when you move on from college, you'll already be prepared to keep your new house or apartment organized. Even if you end up moving back in with your parents for a while, the same old habits you had at home before college aren't going to fly. They aren't going to be so forgiving with the dirty dishes in the sink and the shoes in front of the door. You're not fifteen anymore! Adding just a few simple cleaning rituals to your schedule now as part of your Time Diet will help you be more organized in the long run.

Review

OK, let's review what strategies you've learned to get more work done in a shorter amount of time:

1) Don't waste time worrying and stressing-out. You do have time to get it all done. Remember the story about the two cows faced with a huge pasture of grass to graze? Don't think about it. Just put your head down and start grazing.

2) Eliminate your Time Killers. Time Killers are those little things that distract you from your work without your permission. Getting rid of them allows you to get more focused work done faster.

3) Read and study smarter. Read with pen in hand to stay more engaged with your reading and mark important ideas for quick reference later when you're studying for exams. Learn the material the first time through so you don't waste time going back and trying to re-learn it before the test.

4) Spread out the difficulty with homework. You're more likely to stay motivated if you don't save all your big Meat tasks for the end. The more motivated you are, the faster you'll get your work done.

5) Don't let cleaning chores pile up in your dorm or apartment. Cleaning is a Vegetable task. If you do a little bit each week, but if you let it go for a long time it becomes a Meat task you won't want to deal with.

Remember, in your Time Diet there are two ways to get rid of the extra fat in your schedule: 1) Do less or 2) Do your work more efficiently. Once you've determined that you can't do any less, the best way to do your work more efficiently is to stay focused. Focused work is always done faster and better than unfocused work. The trick is to stay focused each time you sit down to work, not just sometimes. That will help you keep your Time Diet in place not just for a semester, but all through college and the rest of your life.

MAINTAINING YOUR TIME DIET

Emily Schwartz

Congratulations! You now have all the knowledge and confidence you need to begin your own Time Diet. Now, you just need to make sure this is something you don't do for only a few days. You want this to be something you maintain all through college and beyond. To make that easier, we have one last myth to disprove:

Myth #5: I Must Stick to My Choose-To List Exactly

Now that you are a time management expert, you are keeping a monthly calendar and a daily Choose-To List. You are carefully planning out each task and making sure you have a balanced load of Meat, Vegetable and Dessert tasks every day. You have broken up your day into Time Buckets and have chosen tasks for each bucket based on your energy level. You've eliminated all of your Time Killers and have cleared your desk so you can focus on your work. Yes! You're ready to have the most productive day of your life!

....and then the pipes burst above your apartment and flood the whole place, or you catch the flu that's been going around. There goes that plan!

The truth is, life rarely goes exactly according to plan. You can't get too frustrated if you aren't able to stick to your Choose-To List exactly as you planned it. The key is to be flexible and roll with the day-to-day emergencies, both big and small, that may come up.

> ◈ My junior year, during midterms, I came downstairs to find my bike had been stolen during the night. It threw off my whole week! It took three times longer to get everywhere until I could replace it.

Your Choose-To List is a Goal

A good way to get past the speed bumps you encounter during the day is to think of your Choose-To List as a goal, not a list that is set in stone. You have a plan of attack for the day, but if something throws you off, you need to be flexible and take a different path toward your goal. You will have a really hard time maintaining your Time Diet if you get thrown off course too easily when unexpected things come up. Be flexible!

Make it a Habit

Another way you'll be thrown off your Time Diet is if you fail to make the things we talked about in this book a habit. Sure, it's easy to do something once or twice, but making something a habit takes much more diligence. The key is repetition. The longer you stay on your Time Diet, the easier it is to maintain. A good way to form new habits is to combine them with old ones. For example, if you sit down to a bowl of cereal every morning, then compose your daily Choose-To List as you eat your cereal. You can even keep a pen taped to the cereal box if it will help you remember! Combining this new task with an old one that is already routine will help making your Choose-To List become a habit much faster.

> ◈Habits take a long time to form! Don't get discouraged if your Time Diet doesn't feel natural at first. Stick with it.

Tell People

It is much easier to stick to a plan if you become accountable to someone beside just yourself. Tell a friend, family member or roommate about your Time Diet. Don't just tell them it's something you're working on, describe it in detail! Tell them all about your Choose-To List, when you make it and how you follow it. Tell them what your Time Killers are and how you are going to get rid of them. Tell them about your Time Buckets and how they change from day to day. Give them regular updates and encourage them to ask you how your time management is coming along.

Another benefit to telling your friends about your Time Diet is that it's a great opportunity for them to work on their time management as well. Even if your friend looks like a time management pro on the surface, you might not see that he too is struggling to meet his deadlines. Go on a Time Diet together! Having each other as a support system is a great way to stay motivated.

Anticipate Your Struggles

Any college student can tell you that the most hectic weeks of the semester are around midterms and finals. These busy times are when your Time Diet will help you the most, but it's also when you're most likely to slip back into your old habits. Prepare for those crazy times

> ◈During your stressful times, take notes about what you could do ahead of time to make yourself less stressed. Don't just assume you'll remember next time around.

now by making a plan for midterm and finals week before they start. Schedule your test reviews extra early. Make sure to plan Dessert tasks so you won't feel burnt out. You know those will be difficult times, so don't let them catch you off guard.

Celebrate Your Successes

The best motivator to keep up your Time Diet is success. Just like people on a weight diet use the dropping numbers on the scale to stay motivated, people on a Time Diet must rely on their decreased stress level, increased productivity and feeling of control to keep going. When you finish a big paper early for the first time, celebrate! When you get to have a full eight hours of sleep the night before a test because you've learned how to break up your studying, reward yourself! The more success you have with your Time Diet, the more likely you are to keep it going.

You Are in Control

The most important concepts you should take away from this book are that

YOU are in control of your own schedule

YOU have the power to pick tasks for your Choose-To List

YOU have the power to chunk your time into Time Buckets so it is more manageable

YOU have the power to choose a balanced selection of Meat, Vegetable and Dessert tasks

YOU have the power to not waste time stressing out

YOU have the power to eliminate your Time Killers before they waste your time

YOU have the power to put start dates as well as due dates in your calendar

YOU have the power to set your own deadlines so you don't procrastinate

And most importantly....

YOU have the power to cut the fat from your schedule and lead a stress-free college life

Good luck with your own Time Diet. Bon appétit!

Emily Schwartz

ABOUT THE AUTHOR

Emily Schwartz, founder of The Time Diet, is an educator, speaker, trainer and blogger committed to helping people find simple time management solutions. Her trainings have been praised for their creative approach, engaging style and most of all, their results. Emily's background in both K-12 and university-level teaching enable her to make her content both comprehensible and enjoyable. A Southern California native, Emily currently resides in Phoenix, Arizona with her husband Dan and her dog Maggie where she is completing her PhD at Arizona State University.

Make your next meeting or event both educational and memorable with The Time Diet. Emily is available for keynotes and workshops as well as both half-day and full-day trainings. Check out www.TheTimeDiet.org for more information or email Emily@TheTimeDiet.org.

www.TheTimeDiet.org

www.TheTimeDiet.org

Notes